The Official MORK & MINDY Scrapbook

The Official MORK & MINDY™ Scrapbook

By Steven Seabrook

A WALLABY BOOK
PUBLISHED BY POCKET BOOKS NEW YORK

**POCKET BOOKS, a Simon & Schuster division of
GULF & WESTERN CORPORATION
1230 Avenue of the Americas, New York, N.Y.
10020**

ISBN: 0-671-79083-8

First Wallaby printing May, 1979

1 0 9 8 7 6 5 4 3 2 1

Contents

Preface   vii

The Story of Mork   4

Mork Moves In   19

To Tell the Truth   33

Mork Runs Away   47

Mork In Love   63

Mork Runs Down   75

Mork & Mindy's Passport Applications   87

Cora & Fred's Passport Applications   88

Galactic Maze   89

Mork   90

Mindy   91

Cora, Fred, Eugene and Exidor   92

Mork Paper Doll   93

Egg Mobile   94

Orkan Animal Life   95

Grsmbo Passatti   96

Mork Goes Public   97

Old Faces   107

How To Do An Orkan Hand Shake   117

Orkan Flight Ticket   118

The Ultimate Mork Trivia Test   119

Trivia Test Answers   124

Glossary   125

Preface

"Na-No, Na-No"

With these words, a character unlike any other in the history of television entered the lives of millions of Americans. His name, Mork. His place of origin, the planet Ork, billions of light years (sixty **bleems**) from Earth. Emerging from his eggshell-like spacecraft one starry night, this odd but not so strange visitor from another world launched a love affair with countless Earthlings.

He drank through his finger. He sat on his face. He slept hanging from a bar. But, more important, he made a great deal of sense.

Of course, he had some help along the way. He had the good fortune to touch down just outside Boulder, Colorado, at the exact moment that a dazzling and savvy young woman named Mindy McConnell was fending off the advances of a forward young man. She hopped out of the car and found comfort in the just-hatched Orkan. Romances have begun in more peculiar ways.

She wasn't far wrong. The bumbling Orkan ambassador was usually more human than most humans. The lessons this alien taught were not scientific, intellectual or technological, but less exotic concepts, like tolerance, nonviolence and humor, the richest but least-used tools in the human arsenal.

Even Mindy's suspicious father was baffled by the Orkan. This "monster" from outer space could perform the expected parlor tricks on demand — turning himself green, disintegrating objects, tampering with the passage of time — but had no ulterior motives, much less a master plan or death-ray.

Those on the fringes of scientific respectability have frequently postulated that perhaps the human race was founded by such space travellers, that Earth is a colony founded by galaxy-hoppers of a previous era. They spend their time looking for launchpads and cave drawings of spaceships.

If they are right, we might do well to hope that our founding alien fathers bore some Orkan bloodlines and contemplate what's gone wrong in the intervening millennia.

It seems somewhat plausible, for there's more than a bit of Mork in all of us. We don't drink with our fingers (although this would make good sense and facilitate cocktail party conversations) or sit on our own faces. What is it we all share with the Orkan?

Until we crack the riddle, we might do best to study the life and work to date of Mork, which is the subject of the attractive little volume you're reading. Here you will find the stories of Mork's most memorable adventures, scores of pictures from these episodes, and a trove of information never-before seen by human eyes. Finally, you can see how well you've learned your lessons by taking the Great Mork and Mindy Trivia Test, and brush up on your Orkan by consulting the Glossary at the back. You should also play the Orkan maze, hang up the egg-mobile and be nice to your parents.

And you are the recipient of the greatest offer in the history of the written word. This book contains a **completely genuine** ticket for interplanetary travel between Earth and Ork (round trip, of course). Check page 118 of this copy: Unless your ticket has been lost (in which case it unfortunately cannot be replaced), you may proceed to the intergalactic launchpad specified on the ticket and be winging your way to another galaxy before dinnertime.

Na-No, Na-No.

The Story of Mork

September, 1978. A galaxy sixty billion light years away. The planet Ork. The capital city, Frizbat. A large white room, containing no furniture save a stark white desk.

Mork, citizen of Ork, was nervously pacing the room and reprimanding himself. This was the third time he had been called before the "White Desk," Ork's judicial system for petty offenses. On each occasion, Mork had perpetrated a *splink* — a practical joke — which failed to amuse his superiors. His most recent crime: painting a mustache on the solar lander. Mork was startled as a stern voice called out his name. He quickly straightened up, then tried to assume an innocent and casual pose.

"Oh, good morning, Orson." Orson was Mork's superior and now his judge,

and he was in no mood for Mork's special wit today.

"'Orson!' Yes, you call me 'Orson' to my face, but behind my back it's 'Fatso,' 'Rocketship Thighs,' 'Star Tush' and Laser Breath.' "

"I was hoping you'd put that behind you," Mork kidded. "Oops, sorry about that, big fella."

"See what I mean, Mork? These constant displays of humor are not acceptable behavior here on Ork."

"Yes," Mork sighed wearily. He'd heard this speech before. "I guess we are a dull lot."

"Emotions have been weeded out of us for the good of the race . . . and you constantly make jokes. I'm afraid that won't do." Orson's voice changed from reprimanding to relishing.

"But I have a little assignment to straighten you out: There's an insignificant planet on the far side of the galaxy. From the fragmented reports we have on it, the people seem to be . . . welll . . ."

"Real *nimnuls*?" Mork suggested, fearing the worst.

"Exactly. That's why I think you'd fit in there, Mork."

"What's the name of this hell-hole?" Orson replied ominously. "Earth!"

"Earth? I was there once, three *krells* ago. I loved that place."

Orson was not pleased; this was supposed to be punishment, not a vacation. "This is a serious mission, Mork. We want to learn all we can about these primitive societies. Your mission is to report back to me, mentally, once a week."

"You can count on me, Orson!"

The two solemnly exchanged the Orkan salute. Mork gripped his ears and twisted them back and forth in the way a human would twist a typewriter roller.

"Na-No, Na-No."

"Na-No, Na-No."

September, 1978. A galaxy sixty billion light years away from Ork. The planet Earth. A city called Boulder in the state of Colorado. It was nighttime in the countryside just outside the city limits.

Two earthlings sat in an open-roofed jeep, surveying the night sky. It was the third date between Mindy McConnell, 21, and Bill Burns, 22.

"What I like about taking you out, Mindy, is that you don't force me into playing that virile-stud-macho role, you know?"

"I'm glad you feel that way, Bill. Men shouldn't feel inhibited about expressing their poetic side."

"You know what I see when I look at the sky, Mindy? Individual points of desolate, unloved light, so lonely because they can never touch."

"How sad." Mindy thought Bill was dreamy.

"Sometimes," the dreamboat continued, "I see the night sky as a woman, tastefully adorned with sequins. Oh, the Milky Way is a bit garish, but it's Necessary because" — Bill broke off in mid-sentence, focused his eyes on Mindy's leg, and continued in a growling, animalistic voice — "it covers her thighs!" He jumped on the hapless girl, pawing her body and making slurping noises.

Mindy screamed and tried to fight him off. She finally grabbed his hair and pulled him straight up.

"Don't you ever do that again, even if my dress is on fire!"

Bill was angry at this rebuff. "Hey, what is it with you? Three dates — I've done my charming bit, my poetic bit, my sensitive bit — now it's time to rock and roll!"

Mindy was seeing Bill's true character for the first time, and was too furious to notice a large four-foot egg with flashing lights slowly descend and land about fifty feet behind the car.

"I find it hard to jump from poetry to rock and roll!"

"Well if that's the way you feel," snapped Bill, "you can walk home." He pushed Mindy out of the car and drove off in a huff.

A few feet away, Mork from Ork had climbed out of his egg-spacecraft and carefully dusted himself off. From a smaller egg, he pulled out a suitcase, and looked around for the other smaller egg he was expecting. Finding it nowhere, he shook his fist at the sky. "You lost half my luggage. You *nimnuls*!" He then carefully

put on an Earthling suit and tie, overlooking the single fact that he put the jacket on backwards, creating the impression that he was a priest in a clerical collar. He walked over to Mindy, who was sitting forlornly on a rock, and greeted her.

"*Syfnid,* Earthling."

Mindy was slightly puzzled, but quite happy to see a priest. "Greetings, Father. What are you doing out here?"

"This is where I was dropped off," Mork replied naturally.

"Well, I got dropped off, too. You want to hear the story?"

"Sure. Mind if I take notes?"

Mork took out a pad and began jotting notes with his finger. It took Mindy the whole thirty-minute walk back to Boulder to tell her story.

The two arrived at Mindy's apartment, a bright and airy though youthfully decorated second-story of a house. The apartment contained a large living room, Mindy's small bedroom, a kitchenette, and an attic. Mindy was pointing out her stained glass window to Mork.

"Well, now you've seen it all. Thanks for walking me home, Father. I'm afraid I didn't give you much chance to talk."

"*Nap, nap,* it was my pleasure. I was sent here to learn."

"Can I get you anything, Father?"

"Just a glass of water, if it's not too precious. If it is, I'll settle for a quart of oil."

Mindy laughed, thinking her visitor was kidding and went to fetch him the water. As she did, she noticed for the first time why Mork appeared to be a minister.

"Your suit's on backwards! You're not a priest! Who . . . are you?" Mindy was getting scared.

"I'm Mork from Ork."

"Ork?"

"Ork is a planet. You follow the big dipper until it comes to a dead end and then you turn . . . I don't remember."

Thinking her guest crazy, Mindy began slowly backing towards the door and played along. "Right! I have a poor sense of direction myself. Sooo, you're from outer space, huh?"

"Yes. Mind if I take a picture? Here, watch the *flukie!*" Mork touched his fingertips together, producing a flash, and startling Mindy.

"How — how did you do that?"

"It's my Instamatic glove. Some models starting under thirty *brandels.* I'm thirsty!"

Mork stuck his finger in the tea, which began to vanish.

"You — you drink with your finger?"

"Of course. How would you drink it?"

"With . . . my mouth."

Mork was baffled. "Then how can you drink and talk at the same time? It must be drool city."

Mindy was even more frightened now, as she realized that the visitor's story just *might* be true. "Look, I don't know who you are, but there's no such thing as a man from outer space!" She was greatly relieved to hear a knock on the door.

She opened it to find a two-foot egg, which floated into the room while emitting beeping noises. "Aah," said Mork, "my lost luggage."

Mindy was convinced but shocked. "You actually are from . . . out . . . there? An alien? You're not going to hurt me, are you?"

"Hurt? Damaging other life forms is unthinkable to us," Mork calmly explained. "I wouldn't harm a *harf* on your *cholly-cho-cho.*"

Mindy suddenly felt safe. "I believe you."

"My mission here is to observe, Mindy. I can only do that by being one of you. But I fit in, right?"

"Not . . . really, Mork. Listen — I'm as interested in your planet as you are in us. I can teach you how to act 'Earthling' if you teach me about Ork. Deal?"

"*Kerklenik,*" smiled Mork. "By the way, I will be staying here, right? I've heard so much about Earthling hospitality."

"Well . . . you can . . . *temporarily.* But if my father ever finds out . . ."

"'Father'? Oh, yes, what I looked like before. I see: on Earth, a 'father' is a person who wears his coat backwards. On Ork, a person who wears his coat backwards is called a jerk!"

McConnell's Music Store was a schizophrenic establishment, each of its halves reflecting the taste and temperament of its two chief proprietors — Fred McConnell, Mindy's father, and Cora Hudson, Fred's mother-in-law and Mindy's grandmother. The left half of the store was concerned only with "proper" musical instruments and recordings — violins and Wagner, pianos, and Paderewski, harps and Horowitz. The right side of the store was Cora's domain and a good bit trendier — Meatloaf and Moogs, ELP and electronics, Wonder and wah-wahs.

Mindy was the store's third employee. Her main function seemed to be keeping Fred and Cora from going for each others' throats. Her father and grandmother spent most of their time together needling, teasing and insulting each other. It was a modest and well-kept store which struggled to break even and usually did.

As Mindy walked into work the morning after meeting Mork, she saw that the two nemeses were at it again.

"Frederick," Cora said to him sweetly, "let me ask you a question: If you were in heaven and God said to you, 'I will give you a wish: you can be born with either a brain or a rash on your fanny,' which would you choose, dear?"

Frederick was unsure of her drift. "The brains," he answered.

"Good," said Cora, smiling. "I see you've learned by your mistake." Cora strode out of the room triumphantly.

"Mindy," said Frederick, "isn't that your second cup of coffee?"

"My fourth," she replied groggily.

"Were you up late?"

"Uh . . . yes, yes I was. Oh, but Dad, I met the most fascinating person. I was up half the night talking with him."

"*Him?* Half the night?"

"Daddy! The key word in the sentence was 'talking.'"

"I'm sorry, honey." Fred was ashamed. "It's just that you ran away from home only a month ago and — "

"I didn't run away from home," Mindy said wearily. She'd corrected her father on this score many a time. "I got my own apartment."

As the two stared at each other and smiled, Eugene, a ten-year-old neighborhood boy carrying a violin case walked into the store. He had a new friend with him.

"Hey, Mindy, look who I found on the street looking for you!" It was Mork.

"Correction, munchkin-like person," said the Orkan. "I was merely exploring your world."

"He's new in town, Eugene," said Mindy, covering. "Mork, I'll be happy to show you around town after work."

"Work?" The Orkan tried out the sound of the word several times.

"Most people work for a living," Fred pointed out.

"Hmm . . . what a novel concept." Mork's remark instantly made Fred dislike him.

"Is this some beatnik friend of yours, Mindy?"

"Uh, no. Dad, this is Mork. Mork, Mr. McConnell."

Mork gave Fred the Orkan handshake — second and third fingers together, fourth and fifth fingers together.

Fred withdrew his hand in distaste, and Mindy looked embarrassed.

"Mork," she pleaded, "this is my *father.*"

Mork smiled and squeezed his nose. *"Doo-da, doo-da."*

Eugene broke the tension. "I have to go take my violin lesson. Mork, where do you live?"

"At Mindy's place," he replied innocently. "Come by anytime."

As Eugene left, Fred turned slowly crimson-hued and Mindy wished she were anyplace else.

"'Mindy's place?'" Fred was steaming.

"Oh, yes," replied Mork good-naturedly. "We're living together." The hapless Orkan did not realize that this was an Earthling euphemism.

"Living . . . together??!!" Fred by now more closely resembled a beet.

"Mork is a practical joker," said Mindy unconvincingly. She hoped he had bought it.

"Are you sure? He's not staying at your, uhhh . . . and he's not sleeping in your, uh –"

"Daddy! No one sleeps in my 'uh.'"

"Oh. . . ."

"And nobody's sleeping there either!"

That night, Mork decided to watch some Earthling television. He had seen many shows, but only those from the 1950s – it took twenty years for TV waves to reach Ork. But now he was watching an even older Laurel-and-Hardy movie.

"Annhh! Annhh! A pie in the face. How do you Earthlings think of something so original? So unique?"

Mindy turned off the TV. "Mork, we have to talk, so why don't you sit down and get comfortable." The Orkan complied by bending over and putting his face on the couch.

"Mork, can you take some constructive criticism? It's not nice to sit on your face." Mork assumed an Earthling seated position.

"See, Mork, you have so much to learn. You can't even begin to understand the sort of problems you present."

"I realize I do cause problems. The other time I was on Earth I caused big trouble."

"You were on Earth before?"

"Yes, about twenty *lurks* ago. I was there to see my friend, the Fonz. Want to hear the story?" Mindy did.

"I was in a place called Milwaukee. Lots of beer. I made a friend named Fonzie and he got me something called a 'date' with a girl named Laverne. She thought I was weird and then she touched my wrist and I went *crathanza.* I had to have her earlobe. Her lobes were . . . I mean, you just wanted to tweak them."

"Mork, you can't just go around tweaking people's earlobes on Earth. Now, what else have you learned today about Earth?"

"Don't drink with my finger. Don't sit on my face. Don't tell your father we're living together." Mork would not have added the last item had he known Mr. McConnell was outside the front door at that moment, preparing to knock. Instead, Fred waited a moment.

"That's right," Mindy said. "He wouldn't understand."

Fred burst in, furious. "No, I wouldn't!"

"Oh, greetings, Mr. McConnell," Mork said chipperly.

"Mindy!" Fred now looked more hurt than angry. "I wanted to believe you today, and I came here hoping I wouldn't find . . . what I've found."

It was Mindy's turn to be hurt. "You came here . . . to check on me?"

"I came here to prove to myself that my daughter hadn't lied to me . . . that she wasn't living with a man."

"Oh, Dad, it's not that way. . . ."

"Instead, I've proven to myself that my little girl"—Fred was crying—"isn't a little girl any longer." Fred wheeled and walked out the door and Mindy ran to her bedroom crying.

Fred headed straight for the music store, where he spent the next four hours with a bottle of champagne, in his cups and in the dumps. Shortly after midnight, a knock came at the door.

"Fred? You okay in there?" It was Tilwick, the deputy sheriff and an old friend of Fred's.

"Tilwick, come in," Fred mumbled groggily. He was clearly going fast. "Have some champagne. I've been saving it since 1967 . . . for my daughter's wedding, but now . . . Tilwick! A toast to the old days! When values were values and morals were morals . . . when shacking up meant building a hut!"

"What are you talking about?"

"My daughter is living with a man, Tilwick."

"Mindy? Naw, that can't be."

"It's true. I've done my best. There's nothing I can do now."

"Well, there's something *I* can do," said Tilwick. "I'm a cop! I represent law and order! I can go over there and scare the daylights out of the guy. You know, 'Hit the road, Hamburger,' that kind of stuff."

Fred was touched by Tilwick's concern. "You'd do that for me?"

"Sure, I'll go over there tomorrow morning when I'm off duty. First, because you're my friend. Second, because your daughter's only a year older than mine."

Mork had no idea who was on the other side of the door when he heard a knock the next morning. He opened it to see a belligerent-looking deputy sheriff. "Hi, Smoky," drawled Mork. "I'm Mork. *Na-No, Na-No.*" He extended the Orkan handshake. Tilwick was caught off guard for a moment, then resumed his tough-guy manner.

"I'm not a member of your fraternity, kid, so knock off the secret handshakes. Is Mindy McConnell here?"

"No, she's at a place called 'work.' A strange concept, but she seems to enjoy it."

"Oh, and I suppose you don't like work, huh?"

"Wouldn't know. Never tried it."

"I know your type," growled Tilwick. You just live off her. I think you're about the lowest form of life."

"Then you should brush up on your biology," Mork instructed him. "The lowest life-forms are the *Swig, Nelf* and *Hibengie.*"

"Don't pull that intellectual stuff on me. You know, I can make things pretty tough on you. See this uniform?"

"Ah, yes, it *is* a uniform. I was afraid to mention it. Are you . . . Space Patrol?"

Tilwick was beginning to think Mork was crazy. "Are you putting me on, kid?"

"No, it would be difficult to put you on. You aren't even hollow."

"Suuuure. . . ." Tilwick was leery.

Mork leaned over and whispered, "Did Orson send you to help me save my friends, the eggs?" This was a reasonable question to ask someone from the Space Patrol.

"Yeahhh, rigggggght. . . ." Tilwick was now convinced that Mork was crazy. There was only one thing to do — take him in. Tilwick slowly drew his gun. . . .

By the time Tilwick told Fred and Mindy what he had done, Mork's sanity hearing at the city courthouse was already in progress. Fred had not expected such a turn of events; remorseful, he ran with Mindy to the courthouse, swearing that he would do anything to help Mork. They ran into the judge's chambers just as the prosecuting attorney was questioning Dr. Litney, a court-appointed psychiatrist. It

was an informal hearing around a conference table.

"Your honor! Your honor! Stop everything! I'm Mindy McConnell and this is my father. We're here as character witnesses for the defendant." She turned to the defendant. "Mork, I'm sorry we're late, but no one would tell us where the hearing was being held." She turned back to the judge. "I want to go on record as saying that Mork has the right to a lawyer. I will not permit him to be without counsel. It's undemocratic —"

A young man with a hopeless expression on his face stood up and interrupted Mindy. "I'm his lawyer. The court appointed me."

"Oh. . . ." Mindy was deflated. "May I just ask one question?" The judge nodded and Mindy took a folded piece of paper from her purse.

"The question is" — she suddenly was a lawyer — "Mork is innocent! True, he is different from most, *but* — this great country was built on the rights of individuals to be individuals! We have the God-given right to be eccentric and therefore I ask — no, I demand — that Mork be exonerated and set free!" Fred began applauding lustily but tapered off when he saw that he was alone in his appreciation.

The judge was livid. "May we proceed with the testimony of Dr. Litney?"

Mindy sat down, humiliated, as the prosecuting attorney rose to continue his examination.

"Dr. Litney, what were your conclusions after your examination of this patient?"

"He is extremely child-like and incapable of learning. I also found marked antisocial behavior and therefore believe he is incapable of functioning in society."

"No further questions," snapped the prosecutor.

"Right, no questions," said Mork's lawyer. Mindy jumped up again.

"Mork, don't let them do this to you! You don't know what it means."

"I have a vague idea. Last night I was watching *'Perry Mason.'*" The Orkan got to his feet and approached the bench. "Your Honor, I salute you," he said. Then, twisting his ears, he saluted the judge: "*Na-No, Na-No.* In your law, it seems I have a right to speak for myself. I'd like to ask Dr. Litney a few questions." Mork suddenly adopted the character of Spencer Tracy in *Inherit The Wind.*

"Dr. Litney, is it true you don't like me?"

Litney was outraged. "Your Honor, I have *never* been interrogated by a witness before!"

"Then how do you know I'm doing it now? *Annhh! Annhh!*" Mork grew serious again. "You said I was antisocial, Dr. Litney. Why?"

"You wouldn't tell me where you were from," explained Litney.

"You wouldn't tell me where *you* were from," snapped Mork.

"That's not my job."

"Mine, either. Now about those tests you ran that made you hate me. . ."

"Your Honor!" Litney was becoming flustered. "I don't hate the man, but in one test he tried to fit a square peg into a round hole."

"But I did it," Mork pointed out. "And that's why you dislike me."

"I don't have time for this," sneered Litney.

Mork hoisted his pantleg to reveal a watch strapped to his ankle.

"The time is ten thirty-six . . . exactly. *Beep!*"

"See, Your Honor!" Litney sound triumphant. "He even wears a wristwatch on his ankle!"

"No, I wear an anklewatch on my ankle," Mork calmly explained. "If I wore an anklewatch on my wrist, *then* I'd be crazy."

"Your Honor," Litney began, trying another tack. "On the inkblot test, I asked him what he saw." Litney held up an inkblot. "He said it looked like somebody spilled ink! Anyone can plainly see what those two people in the inkblot are doing! And then he flunked the word-association

test outright. That's where I gave him words like . . . oh, I don't know. . . ."

"White?" Mork offered.

"Black, yeah that's it." Litney did not realize *he* was now the patient. Mork continued feeding him words.

"Tall."

"Short."

"Sky."

"Birds."

"Sex."

"Pamela."

The court reporter, a pretty woman in her twenties, jumped up and started screaming hysterically. "Dr. Litney! You said you'd never tell! Never tell!" She began sobbing loudly. The prosecutor looked hurt.

"Litney? Pamela, you and Litney? I thought we . . ." The prosecutor was crestfallen. Pamela ran from the room, still sobbing.

"Your Honor. I have a . . . patient to see," said Litney, running after Pamela. The prosecutor was in close pursuit, and they raced after the young woman and out of the judge's chambers.

Mork had remained calm through all this. "Your Honor," he said, "the defense rests."

The judge looked sternly at Mork. "While it is true that the defendant may add a new definition to the word 'eccentric,' there is no law against that. And since he's no danger to himself or to society . . . and we no longer have a prosecutor or a witness or a court reporter . . . case dismissed!"

Mindy ran over and hugged Mork, and Fred reluctantly offered his hand in congratulations.

The public defender was still in disbelief. "I won? I won!"

Mork walked over to the lawyer and extended the Orkan handshake.

"Na-No, Na-No."

And so Mork came to Earth and was found to be quite sane by the aliens.

MORK'S REPORT TO ORSON

Come in, Laser Breath.

Watch it, Mork. I'm only sixty billion light years away. Just tell me what you've learned about Earth.

Oh, I've learned a lot! Everyone on this planet is an individual. What's more, they're proud of it!

Amazing! How can a society function if everyone's different?

Well, if someone gets *too* different, they're thrown into a place called the "slammer." It's not a nice place. They almost sent me to one because they thought my mind was imperfect.

Aha! So there is *intelligent life on Earth.*

And something happened that confuses me, Orson. I met an Earth girl and her biological father. At my hearing, they came to my defense.

Why would she do a thing like that? She hardly knows you.

I don't know. It must have something to do with emotions.

Investigate the phenomenon closely. It's interesting behavior, even if it is irrational.

Yes, it is. . . . This may sound strange, Orson, but knowing somebody who would do that for me makes me feel . . . really good inside.

Just remember you're there to observe, Mork — not to get involved.

Yes, Sir! Well, this is Mork, signing off from Boulder, Colorado.

Mork Moves In

The morning after Mork's triumphant sanity hearing found Mindy puttering around the kitchen in a housecoat and fuzzy pink slippers. She still couldn't quite believe that a being from another planet was sleeping in her house, but she was surprised at how quickly she was getting used to the idea. It was no different from entertaining the ambassador from a foreign country, she thought to herself, and she felt flattered to have royalty in her home.

Mindy sleepily poured out two bowls of dry cereal and called out to her otherworldly houseguest, "Come and get it! I hope you like corn flakes!"

Mindy was startled to hear a voice coming from the armoire in the corner.

"Why wouldn't I? Just because I'm from another planet, it doesn't mean I'm *that* different," chirped Mork.

Mindy cautiously opened the door to the armoire and was only a little bit startled to see Mork hanging upside down from the clothing bar like a possum.

"Believe me," she laughed, "you *are* different.

The two sat down to breakfast — cornflakes and milk for Mindy, cornflakes drenched in coffee for Mork. Mindy began speaking seriously.

"We have to find you a place to live. You can't go on living here because my father is . . . conservative . . . prudish . . . what's the word I'm looking for?"

"Nerd!" suggested Mork.

That's it," giggled Mindy. "We also have to find you a job."

"But I have a job," said Mork. "I'm supposed to observe everything on earth and report to Orson on Ork."

"I mean a job that pays money," Mindy explained. "You *do* understand the concept of money?"

Mork replied by running to the closet and producing two bags. Picking up one with great pride, he announced, "I've brought with me untold wealth," and poured his treasure on the table.

Mindy stared incredulously. "That's *sand!*"

"That's right. It's been in my family for years."

"But Mork, on Earth, sand is as common as dirt!"

"Oh well," sighed the Orkan. "There goes bag number two!"

Down at McConnell's Music Store, Mindy's grandmother Cora and her father, Fred McConnell, were having their usual morning squabbles. Tiring of the argument, Cora changed the subject.

"Has Mindy come in yet?"

"No, she's probably hanging around with that absurd . . . yo-yo." Fred was no fan of Mork or his strange habits. "I'm scared to death it might become serious. He's already spent the night with her."

"He stayed at her house," corrected Cora. "There's a big difference."

"But that's the first step," complained Fred. "For all I know he's there right now." Fred eyed the telephone and began nervously playing with the dial, dying to call Mindy's apartment. Cora began taunting him.

"You could pick up the phone and find out if he's there in a second."

"No!" said Fred emotionally. "That would be like spying. I could never stoop so low."

"You underestimate your potential, Fredzo—" Before Cora could finish her sentence, her son-in-law was dialing furiously.

The ringing telephone interrupted Mork, who was almost through speed-reading Webster's dictionary, and Mindy, who was hurriedly finishing dressing.

"Could you answer that, Mork?

Taking her at her word, Mork began "answering" the phone—imitating its ringing noise. "No, no, get the phone," said Mindy.

Mork suddenly recalled what a telephone was used for, but he had no idea what it looked like and began tracing the sound to the general vicinity of the kitchen counter. He got no response from the toaster, and finally grabbed the receiver of the phone. The ringing stopped, and Mork looked crestfallen.

"I've killed it!"

Upon hearing Mork's voice, Fred slammed down the receiver angrily. "I knew he was there! I'm going over there, and don't try to stop me, Cora! No one's going to corrupt *my* daughter . . . until after she's married."

Cora shook her head as Fred rushed out of the store.

"He's such a wiener," she sighed.

Fred picked a bad moment to burst into Mindy's apartment. Mork was helping her on with her coat, but to a sudden intruder they looked as if they might have been embracing.

"Unhand that child!" Fred yelled at Mork. "What are you doing here? Don't give me any stories or excuses, I want the plain, unvarnished truth!"

"I spent the night," Mork replied innocently.

"It's not what it seems," Mindy tried to explain. "Mork spent the night here because . . . well, I can't tell you. It's a secret."

"Come now, Mindy, we've never had secrets."

Mindy looked at Mork, who nodded his approval.

"Okay. But you must promise not to breathe a word of this to anybody."

"Okay," said Fred resignedly. "I promise."

Mindy looked around and lowered her voice. "Mork is from Ork," she announced proudly. "It's another planet."

It had not been easy convincing Fred of Mork's alien heritage. The Orkan had drunk juice with his finger (since Orkans long ago realized the need to talk and drink at the same time) but Fred had remained unconvinced until Mork turned himself green. Once a believer, Fred was afraid for himself and his daughter, and was more than willing to give Mindy the rest of the afternoon off to find Mork an apartment.

They had searched without luck however, and Mork was preparing to sleep from a tree in Mindy's front yard when she insisted that he sleep on the sofa like an Earthling.

"It's a flat surface," protested Mork. "Won't I get dizzy?"

"Just go up to the attic and fetch a comforter," said Mindy.

Moments later, Mork returned from the attic with an automobile horn and a moose head.

"Which one is the comforter?" asked Mork. "You know, Mindy, I like your attic."

"But it's dark, dusty, and full of spiders."

"My kind of town. Could I live there?"

As soon as Mork planted the idea, it began to grow on Mindy. "Actually, it wouldn't be so bad if we fixed it up. . . . It would be almost like having your own apartment except—my father. He made me promise to move you out tonight."

Mork saw that there was no compromise possible when it came to Fred, and began packing his belongings.

"You can't go now, Mork. It's cold and raining."

"I'll be fine, I'm into weather." He paused and looked at her. But I *will* miss you."

"Oh, Mork, I don't want you to go! Now that I've met you, I realize how unexciting my life has been."

"The important thing is your relationship with your father," said the wise Orkan. My father was an eyedropper and my mother was a sterile dish. Hard to warm up to them. It's best if I leave. I'll still come by and take human lessons."

Mindy accepted the fact that this was the only solution, but insisted they have a parting drink. "It will have to be ginger ale though, I'm all out of bubbly."

While Mindy poured the pop, Mork picked up the phone and dialed Mr. McConnell's number.

"Hello, Mr. McConnell? Mork here. No, that's not quite right, I'm a son-of-a-test-tube, actually. I just called to say that I don't want to stand between you and

Mindy. I'm leaving and I thought it would be nice if you came over and made up with her. Nice talking to you. Good-bye."

"I feel so bad," said Mindy. She impulsively gave Mork a hug.

"Ooh, you're soft," cooed the Orkan. "I could get to like that."

They separated and clinked glasses.

"Here's to the nicest alien I've ever known," offered Mindy.

"Likewise," toasted Mork. He took two sips and began making peculiar but hilarious noises. "I think I'm *bezurb!* It's the carbonation," laughed the drunken Orkan. "The minute those bubbles hit my bloodstream, I get *Ork-faced.* Goin' home, Momma!" He continued changing from one voice to another, imitating the TV shows whose waves had reached Ork.

"Hey! Don't take away my gusto! Help, I'm meltiiiiinnngg. . . ."

The sudden ring of the doorbell stopped Mindy's laughter. "Oh no!" She panicked. "It's Daddy!" She quickly shooed Mork up into the attic and let Fred into the house.

"Hi, honey. I hate to barge in, but Mork called and it got me thinking about the way I acted. I want to apologize."

"It's okay, Daddy, you don't have to say another thing."

The happy moment quickly ended with a sudden crash as Mork tumbled down the attic stairs, wearing sunglasses and a sombrero.

"Hi, Daddy-O," Mork gurgled. Fred's shock gave way to anger.

"What's he going here?! You broke your promise!"

"But you bullied me into that promise, Daddy."

Mindy debated between reconciliation and argument for a moment, then continued the argument.

"I'm a twenty-one-year-old woman, Daddy, and if I want to keep an Orkan in my attic, I will."

"Well, I don't want you to!"

Mork stumbled over to the moose head and faced it nose-to-nose. "What's your sign, baby?" he asked it.

Mindy continued her tirade, "Don't force me to choose between you and Mork, Daddy."

"I'm forcing you."

Mindy thought for a moment then walked to the door and opened it. "Mork stays. Good night, Daddy."

Fred stormed out with a contemptuous parting look at Mork. "I'm never coming back, never!"

Mindy stood trembling in front of the door. She had never wanted it to come to this.

"I'm sorry," said Mork, suddenly sober.

"You're not drunk anymore!"

"We only stay *bezurb* for sixty seconds. I was out for five minutes, which means I really hung one on!"

Both turned as the door to Mindy's apartment opened. It was Fred.

"On the other hand," he continued as if he had never left, "never is too long a time."

"Oh, Daddy," Mindy cried happily as she went to embrace her father.

And so Mork came to live in Mindy's attic, and Fred learned to live with it.

MORK'S REPORT TO ORSON

Mork calling Orson, come in, Orson.
Orson to Mork. Am I coming in clear?
Too loud! Too clear!

You're coming in fuzzy. What's the matter with your head?

I'm sending fuzzy . . . I'm afraid I got a little *bezurb* last night.

You're supposed to be observing the planet, not running around getting Orkfaced. Have you found a place to stay?

Yes, a cute little place. It's very gloomy and loaded with spiders.

Well, at least you won't get hungry. How's the sand holding out?

Been wanting to talk to you about that, Orson. I found a safe place to put it . . . a cat box.

But that's —

That's what it's worth here, Orson.

Haven't you found out anything important?

Yes. Believe it or not, trees here are green . . . the black liquid is three dollars a pound . . . and it takes two to tango.

I mean something really *important.*

Well . . . remember that girl I was telling you about? She did a very nice thing today. She defended me against her father. That was a brave, kind thing to do. Since she did that . . . I don't know . . . It's like I'm coming down with feelings for her.

Mork! You know emotions are hazardous to your health! Don't start playing around with that stuff!

Oh, no, not me! Trust me, Orson. This is Mork, signing off from Boulder, Colorado.

To Tell The Truth

Mork sleepily climbed down the stairs from his new home, Mindy's attic. He had been enjoying his quarters there for a week now and was getting almost used to the idea of living in a room just like an Earthling. He busied himself in the kitchen, trying to figure out what to do with the fruit-filled doughy objects called Danish when Mindy appeared from the bedroom in a yellow slicker.

"Why are you wearing a rubber coat?" asked the Orkan.

"It's a raincoat to keep my clothes dry," answered Mindy. But Mork, being from an advanced civilization, had a better idea.

"Well, why not leave your clothes here and go naked? That way they'd stay dry."

Mindy never failed to be amazed and amused by the illogical logic of an Orkan. "I don't think so, Mork," she smilingly replied. "I never know when I might have to demonstrate an accordion."

Mork looked confused for a moment, then realized what his pal was up to.

"Ahh, humor!" he said triumphantly, and made the familiar noise Orkans emit in the presence of Earthling humor, a sound not unlike an antique automobile horn. "*Annhh—annhh!*"

"Well, don't worry, Mindy," he said, regaining his composure. "It isn't going to rain today. Orkans are highly sensitive to ions in the air, and the ion ratio today says"—Mork imitated the sound of a radar scanner—"sunny and clear."

Mindy reluctantly took off her coat, and the Earthling and Orkan walked together to McConnell's Music Store.

The pair was startled to hear a blasting jackhammer as they approached the store, almost as startled as they were by the blasting cold inside the record emporium. Cora was shivering.

"Is our rotten landlord trying to break the lease again?" asked an annoyed and chilly Mindy.

"I don't think so," chirped in Mork. "he hasn't even finished breaking the sidewalk." The three of them looked through the window, and saw that the men with the jackhammers were digging an ever-widening hole. They also saw Frederick, who stormed into the room, too angry for more than a single distasteful glance at Mork. "I just came through that obstacle course out front. There's a ten-foot hole! Someone's going to get killed!"

"Wanker doesn't seem to understand that we have another two years left on our lease," protested Mindy.

"And *you* don't seem to understand that if he kicks us out, he can rent to the restaurant next door at double the price. And why is it so cold?"

"He's trying to freeze us out," explained his daughter. "This is the dirtiest trick he's *ever* pulled!"

"No, it's not," said Frederick slowly. A lifetime of hating Arnold Wanker slowly came back to him. "When we were in the sixth grade, he came to the baseball field and gave us all the free lemonade we could drink. *Then* we found out he'd put a padlock on the only bathroom and it cost me two weeks' allowance to buy the key from him!"

"I babysat him when he was five," added Cora. "He blackmailed me out of all my babysitting money!"

"Did he catch you necking with your boyfriend on the couch?" Frederick asked snidely.

"No," Cora responded slyly. She just loved to get Frederick's goat. "That would only have cost me *half* the money!"

Mork had returned to Mindy's apartment a bit early to make lunch for the two of them. He had perfected the bologna sandwich and was experimenting with a new drink — something the Earthlings called "tea." He had filled a kettle with water and put it on the stove about five minutes before. Now, suddenly, a piercing whistle started up from the direction of the stove, frightening the Orkan half to *gorgles*.

"*Necrotons!* Dive!" He hit the floor, then slowly crawled toward the whistling kettle and finally switched off the stove, making the kettle slowly cool and the whistling stop.

"You jive teapot! You'll never sing again!" The moment of triumph was interrupted by Mindy's entrance. She was soaking wet.

"I'd like to talk to you about your 'ion ratio,'" said Mindy, steaming more than the teapot.

"*Annhh! Annhh!* I made it up!" Mork was quite proud of himself. "I knew it was going to rain. I was *splinking*." Mindy was afraid to ask.

"*Splinking*, on Ork, is telling something that isn't true. A practical joke. . . . Humor! *Annhh! Annhh!*"

"Mork," the drenched Earthling began testily, "that is unacceptable behavior on Earth. We call it lying."

"I am sorry you got wet," said the chastened Mork. "Hey, want some lunch," he said, brightly changing the subject.

"Untouched by human hands!"

The afternoon at the music store did not start off well—Mindy's first customer was none other than the detested Arnold Wanker, dispenser of free lemonade and, more recently, the landlord responsible for the ten-foot hole outside and the ten-degree weather inside the music shop. Mindy was ready for verbal battle, but Frederick took the diplomatic, if nauseating, tack.

"Why, Arnold, absolutely wonderful to see you here, isn't it, Mindy?"

"Well," snapped Wanker, "it isn't wonderful to see *you*. I've tried everything thing but tear gas to get you out." Frederick tried to remain conciliatory while trying to look firm.

"Be reasonable, Arnold, I have a lease." A car horn beeped twice outside.

"In a minute!" Wanked yelled outside. "My wife," he explained to Frederick. "I asked her to drive me to a foreclosure this afternoon."

Mindy couldn't pass up the opportunity to be sarcastic. "I guess you need some social life."

Wanker ignored her. "Where's your phone?" Without waiting for an answer, Wanker picked up the wall phone, dialed a number and began screaming.

"I'm getting tired of calling you about this. I want him evicted tomorrow." Mindy was getting angrier and angrier as Wanker continued. "So what if he's ninety years old? Tell him to start for the door today!"

Again, the car horn honked. "All right, you old bat," scowled Wanker in the direction of his wife. "That's the trouble with people. They're too impatient!"

Mindy had had more than enough.

"Mr. Wanker, for years, you've been harassing people . . . evicting people . . . yelling at people!" Wanker turned his back.

Mindy screamed, "You're horrible!" Wanker still did not respond, and Mindy hit him on the shoulder.

Wanker slowly turned, and Mindy's face froze in horror. The force of her tap sent him crashing to the floor—he had suffered a heart attack.

Frederick leaned over to take his pulse, then looked up at Mindy.

"I think," he said softly, "he's dead."

Annie Wanker, wife of the deceased, sat sniffling in the corner of the music store a few minutes later. Frederick and Mindy didn't know what to do to help. Mr. Wanker's body was still lying in the store, in a back room where the paramedics had put it until the mortuary could come.

Mork could not have picked a worse moment to walk in.

"I just finished my report on the pigeons," he announced cheerfully. "They agreed with everything I said."

"Mork—" Mindy tried to break in, but Mrs. Wanker began crying again.

"Who's the grouch?" Mork didn't know any better.

"Shhh!" Frederick interjected. "She just lost her husband."

Mork always liked to look on the bright side of things. "He'll turn up, don't worry!"

"Her husband just *died*," Mindy explained dolefully, quieting and embarrassing the Orkan.

"He was just a wonderful man," cried Mrs. Wanker. "Don't you agree?" She was looking straight at Mindy, who looked at Frederick. Both of them knew it was going to be very difficult to come up with nice things to say about Arnold Wanker.

"Well," ventured Frederick weakly, "he used to give free lemonade to the kids in little league." Although he, Cora and Mindy knew the rest of the story, Annie Wanker apparently did not, for she brightened upon hearing this. Mindy and Cora caught on to his ploy.

"And Grandma said she always wanted to give him things," chirped Mindy.

"*Half* of everything," Cora added quietly.

"Thank you," said Mrs. Wanker. "you've made me feel so much better.

"It's the least we can do for a man who was digging a new wishing well right in front of our store," Frederick tried.

"Not to mention the free air-conditioning," added Mindy, pulling her sweater closed around her freezing body. Now they all began pouring on the half-truths which could be construed as compliments.

"Arnold Wanker was . . . one in a million."

"He was a beautiful man."

"He was an angel."

Overcome with remorse, Mork left the room.

Cora turned to Mrs. Wanker. "Why don't I drive you home?"

41

Suddenly, Mork emerged from the back room, beaming. "Oh, you lucky Earthlings! There's no need to be sad any more. I gave him a jump start!" Mork whistled, and a groggy figure walked into the room—Arnold Wanker!!! Fred and Mindy screamed as Mork began humming "Stayin' Alive."

"It was a one-in-a-million shot," continued Mork. I did it once on Ork to a hairless *gazooba,* but I never dared hope it would work with a lower life-form!"

Frederick whispered to Mindy, "The poor woman. Her only mistake was marrying an idiot."

Wanker began talking as if none of the previous half-hour had passed: "And furthermore, McConnell, I'm going to make you break your lease if I have to break your legs!" The others tried vainly to convince him he had died, but Wanker would have no part of it. He stormed out of the store, vowing vengeance on the McConnells.

"Watch out for the hole!" Frederick warned. . . .

The next day, Mork and Mindy reviewed the extraordinary events.

"Wanker really lucked out, Mork. He took a terrible fall in the hole and only broke both legs and his collarbone."

"But the good news is, he'll be in traction for months," the Orkan slyly replied, then continued in a more serious vein, "I'm sorry about yesterday, Mindy. You all said such nice things about the man, I thought you'd be happy when I brought him back."

"It isn't your fault, Mork. I guess I confused you with my lecture on lying and *splinking.*" Mindy was thinking about how she had gotten drenched because of Mork's *splinking.* "I should have told you about 'little white lies.'"

"All *splinks* are blue," noted Mork.

"Well, I bent the truth a little . . . stretched it a lot."

"Hmm," the Orkan contemplated, "on Earth, the truth gets a lot of exercise."

"Look, as a rule, you should always tell the truth. Okay?"

"Okay," Mork agreed.

The door opened and Cora bustled in wearing a long coat. "Oh, hi kids, I'm going to the Grey Panthers' Prom this Sunday . . . and I want to show you my new dress!"

She took off the coat to reveal the ugliest dress in the free world. She turned and modeled the nightmare as Mork and Mindy stared in horror.

"That's, uh, very colorful," said Mindy, obviously hedging.

"What I *really* want is a man's opinion," said Cora, looking towards Mork.

Mindy leaned over to the Orkan: "*Splink* like you've never *splunk* before," she whispered.

Mork looked up at Cora, took a deep breath, grabbed Cora in an exaggerated Valentino pose and said:

"Oooh, la la! Some foxy granny! Do you come here often? Kiss me, you foolish!!"

And so Mork learned how to tell the truth, Earthling-style.

MORK'S REPORT TO ORSON

Mork calling Orson. Come in, Orson.

I hear you, Mork.

Good evening, Mr. and Mrs. America and all the ships at sea.

Just file the report, Mork.

You take all the fun out of it.

The report, Mork.

Today's report is about little white lies.

What?

It's like little blue *splinks*. There are all sorts of them. For instance, there's a sports lie — 'I tell ya, Harry, ya shoulda seen the one that got away.' Then there are vanity lies — 'I'm only twenty-nine.' Then there's lies to keep from getting your lips ripped of — 'Mighty fine dinner, honey. Who'd believe that's the first meal you ever cooked. Never seen anybody do that with figs before. The secret must be in the cheese.'

That's the way it is on Earth. This is Mork, signing off from Boulder, Colorado.

Mork Runs Away

Mork sat in the chair, afraid and uncomfortable, his hands immobilized under a sheet. He had withstood this for ten minutes and he could take no more.

"That's enough! I'll tell you what you want to know!"

Mindy laughed. Orkans could be such little boys sometimes. "Don't you get haircuts on Ork?"

"No, we have *noggachomps.* They're fuzzy green animals about two inches long. We put them on our heads and let them graze. It's only dangerous if you fall asleep in the chair—a maverick can get loose from the herd and run down your neck. That's why we always set traps in our shorts."

Mindy reacted with mock revulsion, then shook out the sheet that had been covering Mork. "You look much better now," she said, inspecting her work.

Mork proudly drew a roll of bills from his pocket. He knew how Earth worked! "What do I owe you?"

"No, Mork, the haircut's on me."

Mork knew better. "Actually," he said, "the haircut's on *me.*"

Their banter was interrupted by the phone, which Mindy answered.

"Hello . . . Brad? . . . How nice to hear from you again. I thought you were in law school. . . . Already? Congragulations. . . . Tonight? . . . Sure. . . . Seven-thirty. . . . 'Bye."

Mindy hung up, obviously excited. "Mork, I have a date!"

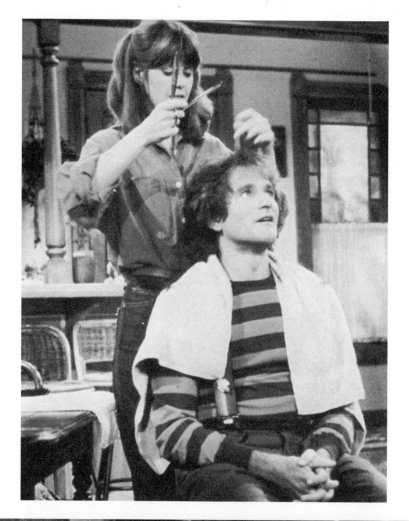

"Don't tell me, I'll guess." The Orkan sat in contemplation for a moment. "June 2, 1852!"

Explaining the difference between friends and boyfriends to Mork had never been easy for Mindy. When she'd told him about her date with Brad, the Orkan had immediately replied, "Good! Where are we going?" Mindy really wanted to see Brad alone; so she strode into McConnell's Music Store with a small brainstorm that afternoon.

"Hi, Mindy," said Frederick. His daughter's reply was almost sickeningly sweet.

"And how's the best, handsomest, most wonderful father in the whole world?"

"Suspicious," said Fred, understandably. Mindy looked hurt.

"Daddy, do you think I want something from you? Well, I'm gonna *give* you something. Two tickets to tonight's basketball game. You're taking Mork." She held out two tickets.

"That's the nicest thing you've given me since the chicken pox," Fred responded sarcastically.

"Fredzo, you're usually not a wiener this early in the day," Cora pointed out.

"But, Daddy, I have a date with a human tonight. It won't be wonderful if Mork's there. That's why you have to take him to the game.

"But, Mindy, I *detest* basketball. How can anyone sit through a game that has so much dribbling?"

"Of course, if I can't date other men," Mindy began with feigned innocence, "I'll just have to settle down with Mork . . . and have a cute little green baby who drinks formula with his finger. . . ."

Before she could say another word, Mindy's father had grabbed the tickets. "Free throw! One on One! Fast break!"

Mindy and Brad returned to her apartment after dinner. He was a handsome sort, impeccably decked out in a three-piece suit. Mindy fetched a bottle of wine and two glasses from the kitchen and poured two drinks as they got comfortable on the sofa. Both were flushed with the exhiliration of seeing each other after so many years.

"Here's to old times," Mindy offered, raising her glass.

"Here's to new times," cooed Brad. The two were already looking forward to many happy and cozy new times together.

"I wish I'd kept in touch with you, Mindy. You're a wonderful girl." Brad leaned over and kissed her gently, only to be startled by a visitor who blithely walked in the front door.

"Greetings," said Mork cheerfully. "Is this the guy you used to like, Mindy?" Mindy and Brad were unhappily surprised by the new arrival.

"Uh, Mork, this is Brad Jackson. Brad, my friend Mork." Brad got up to shake

hands, feeling more than a bit awkward and embarrassed.

Mork naturally extended the Orkan handshake and greeted Brad. "*Na-No, Na-No.*"

"Are you a friend of the family, Mork?"

"No, I just live here." Mork looked at Brad's horrified reaction and wondered why this always shocked people.

"It's not what you think, Brad," Mindy offered weakly.

"Mindy, do you mean he lives with you and you still date other men?"

"Yes, but—" She turned to Mork. "Brad and I haven't finished." She hoped maybe some Earth-tact had rubbed off on her alien housemate.

"Oh, you're still hungry?" Mork sprinted for the kitchen, assuming Mindy was talking about dinner. "I'll whip up my special dessert!"

"Maybe I should leave." Brad stood up.

"Oh, no," Mork offered. "Mindy wants you to stay so we can get to know you better."

Brad was mortified. "Mindy, I don't know what your idea of a relationship is, but I'm not a swinger!" He walked to the door.

"Brad," Mindy tried weakly to salvage something, "I'd like to see you again."

"Oh, sure," he said, obviously not meaning it, "we'll get together soon," and left.

"Hey, wait," Mork called after him. "You missed the bologna sundae!"

Mindy slowly walked to the couch, stared at the two glasses of wine and sat down. She began to cry. Mork touched her face and felt a tear below her eye.

He looked at his finger. He felt awful. "Something has hurt you, hasn't it?"

"Mork, I'm only hurt because he misunderstood our relationship. Ever since you moved in, guys have stopped calling me. I end up not going out and feeling lonely."

Mork was disconsolate. "Is this all because I'm staying here?"

Mindy got up and walked towards her bedroom. "It's not your fault. It was my idea to have you move in. I'll just have to work things out. Good night, Mork."

Mindy awoke the next morning feeling, as one invariably does, much better than she had upon retiring. Now that she thought of it, the encounter between Mork and Brad had been sort of funny. Anyway, if Brad didn't want to take the time to understand that Mork lived with her but was not her lover—well, forget him.

"Hey, Mork," she called out in the direction of the attic. "Breakfast! What would you like? Pancakes? Waffles? Gladiolas? Hey, get up, you lazy Orkan!"

She reached for the stairs and noticed a note pinned to one of the ropes for the attic stairs. She sat down and read it slowly:

Mindy, I Know you are sad because people think you and I are Lovelings. I don't want you to be sad anymore, so I'm going away. If Orkans Knew how to love, I'm sure I would love you, but I don't even understand what love is.

Love, Mork

There aren't many places one can run away to on six dollars, as Mork quickly learned from Eugene, the eleven-year-old sage of the neighborhood. Mork had found Eugene in McConnell's Music Store early that morning; Eugene pleased his parents and tortured Fred and Cora by taking violin lessons at the store.

"You can't even get a place to sleep for six dollars," he had told Mork, "unless you stay in a flophouse."

"Sounds like the perfect place for a flop like me." And so Mork set out for Mission Street, the seediest block in town. The place that caught his eye, understandably, was a crumbling building with a sign saying, "Friends of Venus Headquarters."

The Friends of Venus was not a religious temple, but a cult of believers in UFOs living in one room of a flophouse. Graffiti adorned the walls, expressing such messages as "Martians are Non-Believers." The cult consisted solely of Exidor, who spent his days berating imaginary followers of his cause. Mork entered the room to hear Exidor chewing out his invisible clan.

"Look at you! Eating sandwiches! What's the passenger count now? The ship holds a thousand, and so far we've signed up"—Exidor checked a clipboard—"three. Oh, the pressure of it all, walking the streets, signing up recruits. . . ." Mork took advantage of Exidor's pause to break in.

"Good-bye, I saw your sign outside and thought I might run into someone I knew here."

Exidor was startled, not having had a live prospect in weeks.

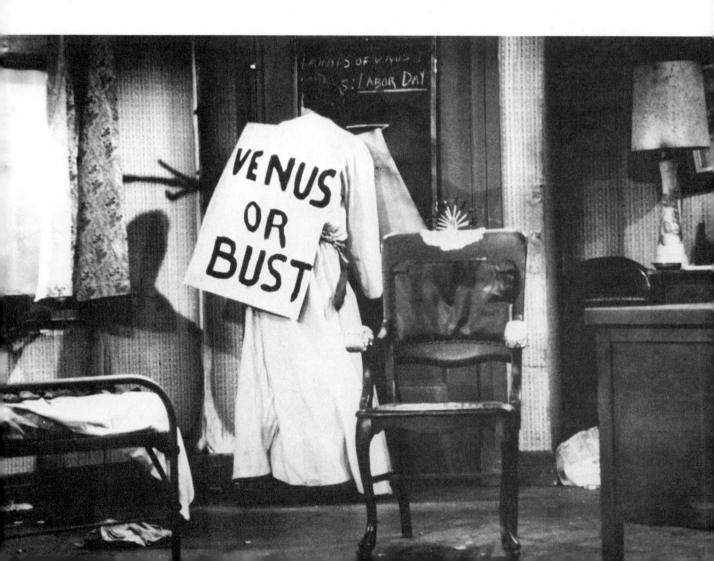

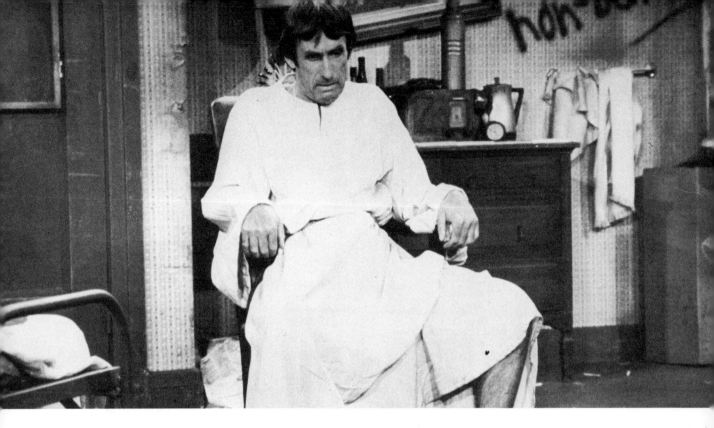

"I know some people from Venus," Mork continued. "I got to know one very well. Cute, if you're into short and fuzzy."

"A believer! A true believer! You believe in people from outer space?"

"What's not to believe?" Mork laughed and extended his hand. *"Shazbot. Na-No, Na-No."*

"Precisely. I'm Exidor. Welcome to the cause." He handed Mork a pamphlet. "This is my philosophy for the Friends of Venus. I want you to study and memorize it, so you can help me convert people to our cause. Now tell me about your meeting with the Venusians on Earth."

"Oh, I didn't meet them on Earth," Mork said matter-of-factly. I met them on Venus."

"You've actually been there?" Exidor was astounded.

"Oh, yes, I've been to all the planets except Pluto. Pluto's a Mickey Mouse planet." Mork quickly flipped the pages of the pamphlet Exidor had given him. "Done," he announced. Orkans are fast readers.

"Exidor, I must talk to you about this philosophy of yours. It's all wrong. First of all, the Venusians aren't going to blow up the Earth. They don't even have the technology for space travel."

"They don't?"

"Let's face it," Mork continued, "their most scientifically advanced invention is the garbage can. They only developed that so that they'd have something to tip over."

"Blasphemy!" shrieked Exidor. "I had high hopes for you, Mork—but you're crazy! I'm getting out of here!" Exidor ran out of the room, brushing by a young woman who was walking towards the door.

"Mork!" the young woman ran into the room.

"Mindy! I didn't want you to find me."

"Well, Eugene finally confessed that you'd gone to Mission Street, and when I saw that sign outside about 'Friends of Venus,' I knew you'd be here. I want you to come home with me."

"No," Mork answered after a moment. "I make you unhappy. You only ask me back because you feel sorry for me. Without me, you're free to do as you wish. You have a home of your own now."

"No, Mork . . . I have an apartment. It was only a home as long as there was someone in it I cared about."

"Me?"

Mindy nodded.

"But I get in your way, Mindy. And when a guy asked you out, I made a real *crilmuck* out of myself."

"Mork, I'm a woman. Sometimes a woman just needs to be held."

"And you wanted that man last night to hold you?"

"Not him necessarily. I didn't really get a chance to find out. Sometimes a hug seems to keep me going."

"Can I try to keep you going, Mindy? I'd hate to see you stop."

He embraced the Earthling in a long and tender hug.

Finally, Mork stepped away. "So soft. . . . It doesn't make sense, but I think I understand why this keeps you going." He paused for a moment, then said, "It's got me going and I don't even know what it is!"

And so Mork came back to live with Mindy and, just as importantly, learned how a hug can keep you going.

MORK'S REPORT TO ORSON

Mork calling Orson. Come in, Orson.

What a terrible connection. It sounds like someone stepped on a frenkle's tail.

It's just me, reporting from Earth.

And what words of wisdom are you transmitting across the Universe today?

Well, I learned how to make a human happy. I learned how to give a hug.

And a hug is?

It's when you wrap your arms around somebody human's body and squeeze.

I thought that's what Earthlings call 'wrestling.'

In wrestling you squeeze a lot harder.

Hugging. Hmmm. Amazing what pleases the primitive tribes. I'll never understand them.

But, Orson . . .

Yes?

It was good for me, too.

Mork!

Yes, sorry, Your Immenseness. Well, this is Mork, signing off from Boulder, Colorado.

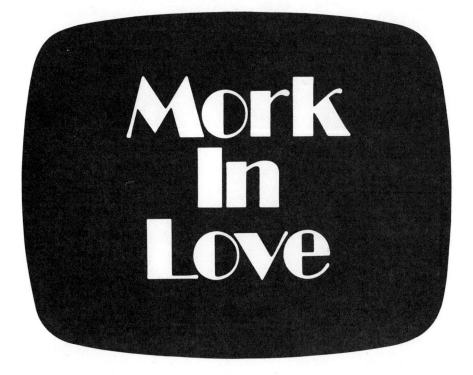

Mork In Love

It had been a week since Mork had returned home — not to Ork, but to his Earth-home, Mindy's apartment. He was coming home today from an afternoon of observing traffic for one of his reports to Orson on the strange customs of this planet. He entered the apartment and, after a few words with his spacesuit, greeted Mindy.

"Mork, you talk to your spacesuit?"

"Certainly. It spoke first. I would be rude not to reply. It's made up of billions of tiny living cells. You primitive Earthlings will learn that life exists throughout the Universe as you gain higher intelligence and sophistication."

"Okay. . . . Well, what did you think of the traffic?"

"I didn't understand. Why do they call it 'rush hour' when nothing moves? I went to a movie instead. It was called, 'Here Comes the Fleet.'"

"Oh, I loved that one," said Mindy.

"Well, then maybe you can answer a question: the first time Biff and Margie met, they got into a fight. In the next scene, they were on a date. Why?"

"Because they were in love, Mork."

"What is this thing called love? I know that it's an emotion, but on Ork we did away with emotions a million *bleems* ago."

"Mork, if you want to experience life as an Earthling, you'll have to experience love."

"Does love lead to mating?"

"Yes," Mindy replied cautiously.

"Oh, Good! I've been wanting to try that! When do we start? We'll have a mating and I'll put it into my next report to Orson, complete with slides and pictures."

Mindy was beginning to feel trapped. "Mork . . . it isn't that easy. I mean love . . . when a man and a woman deeply care . . . that is—"

An urgent noise came from the direction of Mork's spacesuit, which was hanging in the closet.

"Mindy, I don't mean to be rude, but my suit needs me. Can we discuss this love some other time?"

"Whew," said Mindy in relief, "I guess your suit really got me off the hook."

Mork looked confused for a second, then realized what Mindy was up to.

"Ahh, humor! *Annhh! Annhh!*"

The following morning found Cora joylessly dusting off the new window display at the music store, a winsome blond mannequin which she hated almost as much as Frederick liked. He also liked rubbing in how much Cora hated the mannequin.

"Ah, Cora, it does my heart good to see you tending to my inspired window display. Has she attracted many customers today?"

"Customers, no. Dust, yes," Cora snapped. "And I'll tell you another thing, Fredzo—I'm getting a little tired of picking dead flies out of her wig!"

"Have your little jokes, Cora, nothing will upset me today." He pulled a bankbook out of his pocket. "Do you see this? I've scrimped! I've saved! I've done without! But it was worth it. I've got twenty-three hundred dollars in here, just enough to swing the deal. I'm getting a Cadillac!"

"Fredzo, why do you need a car three blocks long when you only live a block and a half from work?"

"I don't need that car to get to work—I need it to get to my high school reunion Saturday night, fifty-three miles from here."

"But I thought you hated high school."

"I didn't hate high school," corrected Fred, "I hated Forrest Collins. He was a big bully and he said I'd never amount to anything."

Cora was touched by this side of Frederick. "Elizabeth never told me any of this."

"That's because I never told her, even though she was my wife. I've never told anyone. . . ." Fred paused in reverie, then quickly continued, "But that's all behind me now! I've saved my money! I'm getting my Caddy! Nothing can ruin my happiness!"

At that moment, Mork walked in, "Hi, Daddy!"

"Except that!" Frederick scowled at Mork and left the room. Mork turned to Cora.

"Hello, Mrs. Hudson. Is Mindy in?"

"No, she'll be back in a while." Mork idly picked up the feather-duster from the table. "Ahhh! A one-legged *hibengie!* I thought they were extinct. . . . Ah, Mrs. Hudson, may I ask you a personal question?"

"Shoot," said Cora.

Well, how do you know when you meet a person you're going to fall in love with?"

"Mork, I promise you . . . when you meet the right person . . . you'll *know.*"

"Then you knew the minute you met Mr. Hudson?"

"Oh, yes," Cora replied dreamily. "It took us fifteen years to realize it was love at first sight."

Mindy had run home from work to pick up the morning mail, for she expected a crucial letter to arrive any day now. Mindy had applied to a journalism school and was waiting to hear whether she had been granted the scholarship which would enable her to go. She tore open each letter, finally reaching the one she had so eagerly awaited.

It was bad news.

As she read it for the fourth time, just to make sure the worst was true, Mork entered in high spirits.

"Hello, Mindy!" He was making strange faces and looking in the direction of the door, which he had left open.

"Mork, what are you doing?"

"Making a fool of myself. But I understand that is normal under the circumstances."

"What are you talking about, Mork?"

I took your advice and went out and fell in love. She's beautiful!"

"Well, I'd like to meet her sometime." Mindy's mind was still on the letter, not on Mork's new romance.

"Well, no time like the present. She's waiting in the hall." Mork walked to the hall and returned with his new amour.

"Mindy, meet Dolly." Mindy's face dropped in sheer shock.

Dolly was the mannequin from the music store window!

Mindy had been sitting aghast for five minutes now, watching Mork fuss over Dolly, make one-sided small-talk and whisper sweet nothings into her wooden ears. Now he was doing a spirited tango to "La Cumprasita," wheeling Dolly around the living room floor. Mindy had seen enough, and angrily switched off the music.

"Mork, you can't have a relationship with a mannequin!"

"Why not? Dolly is beautiful, shy, quiet —"

"Of course she's quiet! She can't talk! You can't love an inanimate object."

"But you once said you loved your book, Mindy."

"That's different."

"And you said you loved 'Here Comes The Fleet.'"

"That's different, too!"

What about my love for Dolly? Isn't that different?"

"That's too different." Mindy got up and stormed out, leaving the lovebirds alone.

Fred was shaking his head in disbelief, as he had been for most of the day. "What kind of a ding-dong would steal a mannequin from a store window? Oh, well, Cora, I'm not going to let it upset me. This is Fred C. McConnell's big day! I pick up my new Cadillac in an hour."

Mindy entered the store, clearly distraught. Immediately Cora asked her what was wrong.

"I wanted to surprise you two. I wanted to go back to college, but I didn't get the scholarship and I can't afford the tuition."

This is kind of . . . a dream of yours?" Fred asked.

"Yeah, I guess it is."

Fred spoke slowly. "I know what that's like, Mindy. . . . Uh, how much money do you need?"

"The scholarship was for two thousand dollars." Mindy walked away to the counter and stood there sadly. Behind her, Fred took out his bankbook, looked at it for a long moment, then walked over to Mindy. He tried to sound suddenly gay.

"Boy, Mindy, this is your lucky day! I'm going to surprise you. Honey, I've been putting a little money aside for you ever since you were a baby. I was going to give it to you when you needed it, and, well, it looks like you need it now."

"What???" Mindy was shocked.

Frederick handed her the bankbook. "It's twenty-three hundred dollars. I wish it could be more."

"This is incredible!" Mindy ran and hugged her father.

"I'll second the incredible," said Cora, genuinely moved.

"Daddy, you're wonderful! I'm going to sign up right now!" She hugged Frederick again and ran out the door.

Cora stood looking at Fred with new-found admiration. "That was a wonderful thing you just did, and I'm hacked off about it. Just when I'm convinced you're an absolute wiener, you turn around and do something nice."

Fred was absorbed in his thoughts. "Did you see the look on Mindy's face? Anybody that can make another human being look like that, he's a success. I can go to that class reunion with my head held high in my old car . . . if I can get it to start."

Later that evening, Cora had made a trip to Mindy's apartment and told her and Mork of Frederick's generous sacrifice. She was just finishing and preparing to go.

"Mindy, you've made him happier today than any car could have. And you can make me happy by not telling him that I blew the whistle. Deep down I know he loves me, and I don't want anything to break up our rotten relationship." Cora smiled and left.

"I find this all rather puzzling," said Mork. "Your father says bad things about Mrs. Hudson, makes fun of her, calls her names, and yet he loves her."

"Daddy and grandma need each other, Mork. That's what love is all about."

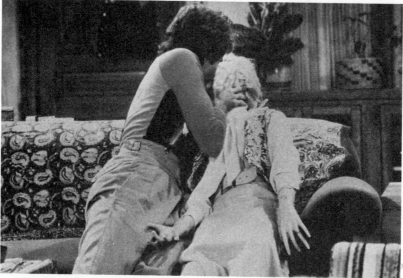

"Ahh, just like my love for Dolly."

"I don't know about the rest of the Universe, but here on Earth there's a big difference between a mannequin and a woman. Mork, go get Dolly." Mork fetched his wooden love from the armoire.

"Now, hold Dolly's hand."

"Mmm, nice."

"Now, hold my hand."

"Mmm . . . even nicer! And your fingers separate."

"Now, a hug."

Mork hugged Dolly, then Mindy. "Mmmm, you're much nicer," he said to his human companion. And no dead flies in your hair!"

"Now, Mork, kiss Dolly."

He did, then gently kissed Mindy. Both were genuinely affected by the kiss, and Mork jumped up.

"Genetic memory! Primitive and wonderful stirrings! I know now what I must do. Mindy, please leave us alone."

Mindy put on her coat and walked out the door as Mork approached Dolly, assuming the attitude of the suave, Continental screen lover about to dismiss his paramour.

"Dolly, I'd like to have a talk with you. . . . Where I come from, there are no emotions. Then I met you . . . I felt about ten *zerks* tall . . . the elegant way you sat up so straight . . . the way you looked me in the eye without blinking . . . I thought I loved you, Dolly, and perhaps in my own way I did. But it's not real love. We can't share our pain, our joy, our needs. We're from two different worlds."

He took her hand. "I guess this is farewell." Dolly's wooden hand snapped off into his grasp.

"Oh," said Mork, quite seriously, "you didn't have to give me back the ring."

And so Mork learned about love.

Mork calling Orson. Come in, Orson.

This is Orson. What's the matter with you?

Me? Nothing.

You've got a strange look on your face.

Maybe it's love.

Love?! Isn't that an emotion?

It's a many-splendored thing. It makes the world go round. It will keep us together. It's all you need.

All I need is a report that makes sense.

Love doesn't make sense — that's why Earthlings think it's wonderful.

Is there anything similar to it on Ork?

No. What happens is that you get hot and sweaty, you can't sleep, you can't eat and you feel dizzy all the time.

It sounds like that disease you got on Venus.

Yes, Venusian's Revenge.

We Orkans made the right decision in giving up emotions.

I'm not sure, Orson. We may have given up too much. I'm more advanced than these humans, yet sometimes I feel so primitive.

I'm afraid I don't understand.

I don't either, Orson . . . but I'm not afraid. Well, this is Mork, signing off from Boulder, Colorado.

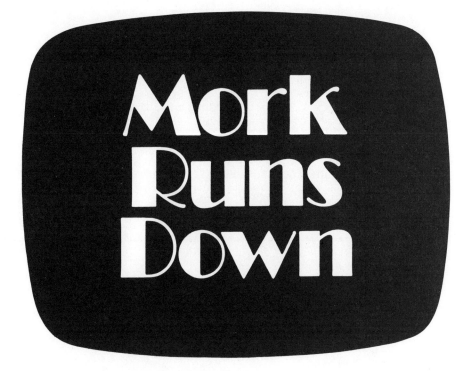

Mork Runs Down

Mindy always enjoyed seeing old friends, and Joyce Rappaport was a particularly old and close one. She had popped in unannounced, but Mindy didn't mind the intrusion at all.

"Joyce, it's really good to see you again. So much has happened."

"Yeah, like my name isn't Joyce anymore. It's 'Rainbow.'" Mindy looked at her old friend and decided that the name-change was wholly in character; Rainbow had frizzy hair, granny glasses and the general appearance of a vintage hippie caught up in a time warp.

"Well, can I get you some coffee, Rainbow?"

"Oh, no, I never drink caffeine."

"A soft drink then?"

"Mindy! Sugar is suicide!"

Mindy felt at a loss. "Water?"

"No, it's full of fluoride. But I'll take a beer. It's got chemicals, but after a six-pack, who cares?"

As if sent to answer, Mork strode in the door at that very moment. "Hi, Mindy. Hi, other person."

Mindy came back from the kitchen with coffee for herself and the beer for Rainbow. "Oh, Mork, this is my old friend Rainbow."

"Na-No, Na-No," the Orkan greeted her."

"Wow, like I like him already," purred Rainbow.

Mork's been having trouble finding a job," Mindy explained.

"Really? Hey, I run a health food store, and I've been looking for a revolutionary stockboy. Are you interested, Mork?"

"Does a Martian have eight legs?" This was Mork's way of replying in the affirmative.

"Terrific! Why don't you come by tomorrow afternoon at one o'clock and I'll try you out. I have to be going." Mindy walked her to the door and they exchanged farewells.

"Later, Mork," called Rainbow.

"Yeah, later, Rainstorm," the Orkan replied.

Mindy shut the door and walked back to mork. "It's Rain*bow,* and aren't you excited? You might have a job!"

"And I thought tomorrow was going to be horrible. It's my birthday," Mork said sadly.

"Horrible? Why, Mork?"

"Birthdays are very traumatic for Orkans because—"

Rainbow came back into the room. "I forgot to tell you, Mork—it's the Vitamin Vendor on Pearl Street."

"Oh, I know the place. It's the one with the winos hanging around in front."

"Yes, but they're vegetarians," Rainbow pointed out. "They never drink wine made from meat."

The next morning, Mork found himself feeling out of sorts. Several times he thought he heard the phone ringing, only to pick it up and hear a dial tone. It oc-

curred to him that it may be time for his recharge.

Mork walked to the armoire and pulled out an egg, which lit up weirdly. "Ahh, my little *gleek,* it's recharge time." He tapped his head with the egg, but nothing happened.

"Hmmm, maybe it's not time yet," Mork checked the anklewatch. "I'm not due for two more hours." He set the alarm on his watch, and placed a note in the watchband, reminding himself what to do when the alarm went off. At that moment, Mindy came into the room.

"Mork, what's that rope around your neck for?"

"It serves a definite purpose, but I can't remember what." It was obvious to Mindy that something was wrong with the Orkan.

"Mork are you all right?"

"No, I had a rough night. I tossed and turned the whole time. And that isn't easy when you sleep hanging from a bar. I think I'll go take a nap."

As Mork walked up the stairs to the attic, Mindy noticed his *gleek*, now unlit, lying on the table. Puzzled, she put it in the egg tray of the refrigerator, then left the apartment.

Mork came back down the attic stairs a few moments later. "I wish I remembered what I was supposed to remember. . . . My *gleek*! If I don't recharge with my *gleek*, it'll be a disaster. My body slows up, then speeds up and then . . . I can't remember. . . . What was I talking about? . . ."

Mindy and Fred were surprised to see Mork walk into the music store two hours later. "What are you doing here?"

"I thought I had an interview."

"Yes," Mindy replied, "at the Vitamin Vendor."

"Oh. When I left the house I didn't feel too good."

"You look fine now, Mork," said Fred.

Well, it comes and it—" Mork seemed to fall asleep in midsentence, then suddenly began jogging around the room.

"Mork, are you sure you're okay?" Mindy was getting worried.

"Who me?" He quickly spun around as if someone had tapped him on the shoulder. "I'm fine. Caw! Caw!" Mork stopped imitating a crow and again seemed to fall asleep."

"I think he needs a doctor, Dad," Mindy whispered.

"You're right, Mindy. There's a doctor in the mall. I'll get him." Fred sprinted out the door and Mork snapped to attention as if he heard a ringing sound.

"Don't answer it, Mindy. I've been imagining a telephone all day."

"It's your anklewatch, Mork." She lifted up his pantleg and shut off the watch. "Hey, what's this note stuck in it?"

"Must be a footnote," quipped the wobbly Orkan. "Oh, I remember, it's the note I wrote to myself this morning. Read it."

Mindy read aloud, "Dear Mork: Just remember. If you don't use your *gleek* in an hour, you'll be dead. Love, Mork."

Mindy wheeled to ask him for an explanation. Mork simply smiled and collapsed.

Luckily, for the moment, Mork revived within two minutes. Mindy knew she was racing against time now, and began questioning him quite rapidly.

"Mork, what's a *gleek*?"

"I . . . I don't know." He was clearly still in a haze. "Wait — *gleek* . . . that was in my note."

"Yes, Mork, *why* did you write that note?"

"What note?"

"This note! Here, in your handwriting!" Mork quickly read the note.

"I'm going to die? Well, it was nice knowing me. Heavy sigh. Deep grief. Well, I'd better grab for all the gusto I can. This next hour's going to be a real *durkiss*." Before Mindy could stop him, Mork jumped to his feet, spun around twice and ran out of the store like a man possessed. A moment later, Fred rushed into the store.

"Don't worry, honey. The ambulance will be here in a minute."

"But Mork's gone!"

"Where?"

"Well, he might have gone back to my apartment . . . or he might have gone to the Vitamin Vendor."

"Right!" said Fred, taking command. "Let's check both!"

Mindy's second thought had been the correct one, for at that moment Mork walked into the Vitamin Vendor, where he was greeted by Rainbow.

"Hi, Mork, you here about the job?"

"No, what are they saying?" babbled the Orkan.

"Ooh, I can dig your essence. Hey, here's a customer. Let me see how you wait on him."

Mork stood still. "How long should I wait?"

"Oh, wow, like time is irrelevant and irrelevant is money. Just go see what he wants."

Mork rushed over to the customer. His movements were growing faster by the moment. "What do you want?" he asked brusquely.

"Do you have any wheat germ?"

"I hope not," snapped Mork.

"Well, my doctor says I need more iron. What do you recommend?"

"Eat your car keys." Mork was getting more and more nervous and agitated.

"Look, do you just have some clover honey?"

"I'll have to check, sweetheart."

The customer stared in disbelief, but proceeded to see just how far Mork would go. "How about some B-12?"

Mork held out his hands and began making airplane noises. "Too big to fit into the store." At this, the customer gave up and called Rainbow.

"Hey, Mork," she said, "something's really wrong with you. Look, why don't you just unpack those brown eggs over there."

Mork looked at the eggs on the counter and snapped back to reality. "Gleeks! Recharge! I need my *gleek!*"

At that instant, Mindy ran in. "Mork!"

"*Gleek!*" Mork was standing stiff as a board.

"I think your friend's been getting too much starch in his diet," Rainbow suggested to Mindy.

"I'm taking him home," Mindy said.

The two reached Mindy's apartment a few minutes later and found Fred frantically dialing the phone. "Why'd you bring him here, Mindy? I thought you'd go straight to the hospital."

"He insisted on coming home. He said he had to get something . . . it sounded like 'gleep.' "

"*Gleek!* Gotta get my *gleek*," yelled Mork.

"We have to find out what a *gleek* is," Mindy observed. "What time is it?"

Fred checked his watch. "Two-thirty."

"We have to find out in ten minutes," said Mindy solemnly. "Mork, you've got to help us. What's wrong with you?"

"It's my birthday," he replied weakly. On Ork, birthdays come only once every two thousand *zymes*. And when they do, our bodies go *zazbat* and we get the *gorgles.*"

"*Gorgles?*" asked Fred.

"It's what you Earthlings call dying." Mindy and Fred looked horrified.

"Look, Mork, what's a *gleek?*" Fred asked. "What does it look like?

Mork's voice suddenly slowed down to an incomprehensible pitch. He struggled to form a word, then finally managed one clear cluck.

"A *gleek* is a chicken?" Mork nodded that Fred was on the right track, then feebly pointed to Fred's bald spot.

Mindy thought she had the answer. "A *gleek* is a bald chicken?"

"No, you egghead," said Fred excitedly. "It's an egg!"

Mork managed to nod.

"I found an egg on the counter this morning," said Mindy, running to the refrigerator as she spoke. She ran back to Mork with the open carton of eggs.

"Which one is it?" she asked. Mork grabbed one and banged it against his head. It splattered. He grabbed another and it too splattered. Mindy began handing him eggs, and he smashed them all against his head, his arms and all over his body. He was rapidly losing control.

Finally, he grabbed the last egg, which lit up when he touched it. He banged it against his head — it didn't break — and he collapsed to the floor in a heap.

"Oh my — Mork? Daddy?" Mindy feared the worst.

Suddenly Mork jumped up, his old self, and gave a big, cheery smile.

"Greetings! Any calls for me while I was out?"

And so Mork ran down and almost got the *gorgles*, but was saved by his *gleek*.

MORK'S REPORT TO ORSON

Mork calling Orson. Come in, Orson.
So what did you learn this week?
Orson, my birthday was this week.
Oh, I'm terribly sorry. My condolences.
Thank you. Earthlings actually celebrate theirs. They even say 'Happy Birthday.'
That's disgusting!

Well, here they all feel really good on their birthdays, Some people like them so much they celebrate the same one over and over.
How did they celebrate yours?
It was a strange ceremony. Mindy brought me a cake, but it caught on fire.
What did you do?
You know me, I'm a fast thinker. I stomped it right out.
Good work, Mork.
Thank you, Orson. Well, this is Mork, signing off from Boulder, Colorado.

UNITED STATES GOVERNMENT
OFFICIAL APPLICATION

For interplanetary travel between Earth and Ork.

(To be filled out by U.S. Government interviewer)

Name _____ Mork XXX (refused to divulge last name) _____

Address _____ 1619 Pine Street Apt. XXTHC _____

_____ Boulder, Colorado _____

Telephone _____ (3 XX O3) 555-1575 _____

Date of Birth _____ 9 bleams ago _____   Height: _5' 10"_

Place of Birth _____ Laboratory Number "gee" _____   Weight: _150_

Marital Status _Single_   Eyes: _Blue_

Occupation _____ XXXXXXXXX Observer, Commentor _____   Hair: _Synthetic_

Aliases _Humphrey Bogart Walter Winchell John Wayne Vincent Pri..._

Characteristic Sayings _"Nanno-nano." "Shazbat." "You thank." "I have to think_ this under."

Other Identifying Features _Claims he drinks with finger, pours coffee on cereal,_ talks to eggs.

Why applicant would like to travel between Earth and Ork _Says he "wants to go home"._

UNITED STATES GOVERNMENT
OFFICIAL APPLICATION

EO-7242920

For interplanetary travel between Earth and Ork.

(To be filled out by U.S. Government interviewer)

Name _____ Mindy McConnell _____

Address _____ 1619 Pine Street _____

_____ Boulder, Colorado _____

Telephone _(303) 555-1575_

Date of Birth _____ October 8, 1955 _____   Height: _5'6"_

Place of Birth _Boulder, Colorado_   Weight: _120 lbs_

Marital Status _Single_   Eyes: _Green_

Occupation _# Salesperson -- Music Store_   Hair: _Auburn_

Aliases _____ The Catwoman from Mars _____

Characteristic Sayings _"That's sweet." "Tell me all about it." "Daddy, I'm 22_ years old!"

Other Identifying Features _Has generally pleasant and easygoing manner; frequently_ jealous of other women; whines and plays with XXX hair when upset.

Why applicant would like to travel between Earth and Ork _Says she wants a career in_ journalism, and would like to report about planet ORK.

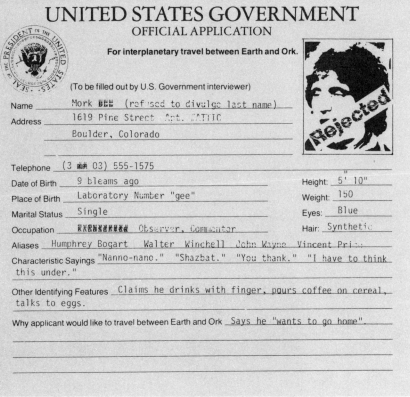

UNITED STATES GOVERNMENT
OFFICIAL APPLICATION

For interplanetary travel between Earth and Ork.

(To be filled out by U.S. Government interviewer)

Name ___ Cora Hudson ___

Address ___ 135 West Avenue ___

___ Boulder, Colorado ___

Accepted

Telephone ___ (303) 555-0694 ___

Date of Birth ___ (applicant refused to divulge) ___   Height: 5' 4"

Place of Birth ___ San Diego, California ___   Weight: 125 lbs

Marital Status ___ Single (widowed) ___   Eyes: Blue

Occupation ___ Co-owner, salesperson, Music Store ___   Hair: Silver

Aliases ___ ~~B###~~ Grandma   Foxy ___

Characteristic Sayings ___ "Don't be such a wiener." ___

Other Identifying Features ___ Enjoys loud electronic music, gin rummy, annoying son-in-law. ___

Why applicant would like to travel between Earth and Ork ___ Wants to see new planet to avoid boredom, see new things, avoid something called "wieners". ___

UNITED STATES GOVERNMENT
OFFICIAL APPLICATION

For interplanetary travel between Earth and Ork.

(To be filled out by U.S. Government interviewer)

Name ___ Fred O'Donnell ___

Address ___ 135 West Avenue ___

___ Boulder, Colorado ___

Accepted

Telephone ___ (303) 555-0694 ___

Date of Birth ___ March 17, 1922 ___   Height: 5' 9"

Place of Birth ___ Las Vegas, ~~Nev~~ Nevada ___   Weight: 160 lbs

Marital Status ___ Single (widower) ___   Eyes: Brown

Occupation ___ Owner/Manager Music Store; Orchestra Conductor ___   Hair: NO

Aliases ___ Fredzo from Scherzo   The wiener ___

Characteristic Sayings ___ "That's the most insulting thing I've ever heard." "No, that's the most insulting thing I've ever heard." ___

Other Identifying Features ___ Develops allergic reaction to popular music; protective of daughter; perpetually worried about business. ___

Why applicant would like to travel between Earth and Ork ___ Says he wants to bring classical music to far corners of ~~te~~ the universe and find eligible potential husband for daughter. ___

Mork

Mindy

Eugene

Fred

Cora

Exidor

Orkian underwear

Ork dress suit

Earth shoes and socks

Ork hat

pin

pin

pin

big bow tie

right-hand glove

Earth shirt

Earth pants with snappy suspenders

ankle watch

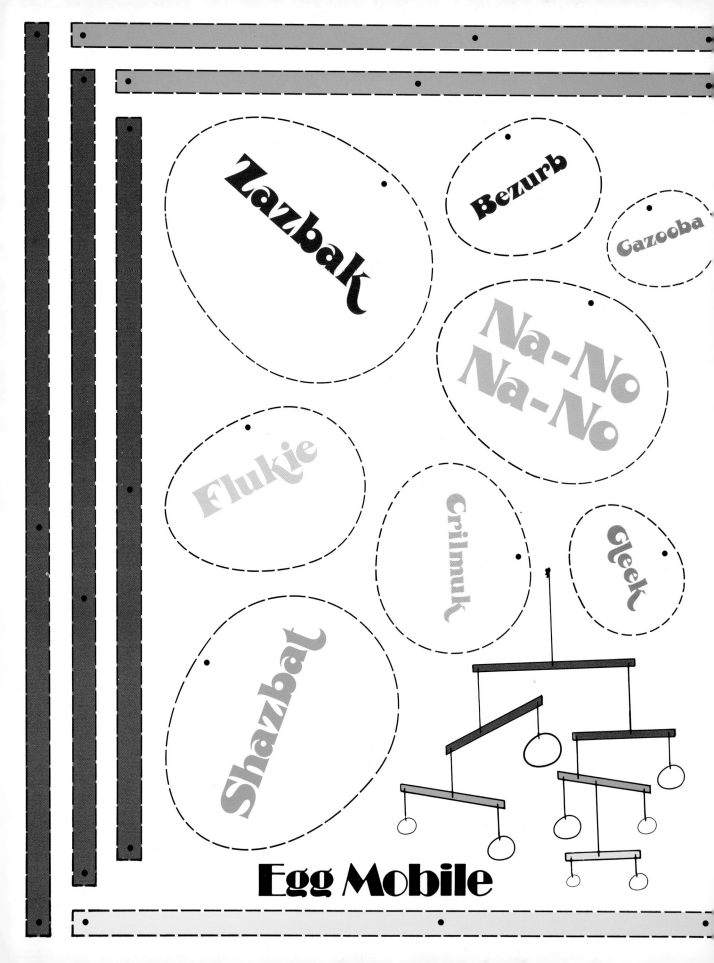

Zazbak

Bezurb

Gazooba

Na-No Na-No

Flukie

Crilmuk

Gleek

Shazbat

Egg Mobile

Mork Goes Public

Business never actually boomed at McConnell's Music Store, but it had slowed to an absolute crawl of late. Mindy and Cora were minding the shop during Frederick's lunch hour one day, and the only other person in the store was Mork, who was listening to "Marcel Marceau's Greatest Hits" through a headset.

"Well, business is really picking up," sneered Cora. "The last couple that walked by the window actually came to a full stop before moving on."

"I feel really sorry for Dad," said Cora.

"Me, too," added Mindy.

Mork had finished listening to the record. "Why are we eating our hearts out for Dad?" he asked.

"Business is the pits," Cora pointed out for the fifth time that hour.

"And on top of that," Mindy informed him, "the water pipe broke in his house and flooded the living room. It's costing him three thousand dollars to fix everything. Well, Cora, let's do those invoices. Mork, would you watch the store while we're in back?" The two women exited and Mork's first customer walked in, a good-looking man in his twenties.

"Are you here to buy an album? If you buy one, I'll give you the chance to buy another at the exact same price."

The customer laughed. "Actually, I'm here to gather some serious information." His tone changed to that of an earnest inquisitor. "Do you know one Mindy McConnell?"

"Yes, I know one," answered. "Are there more?"

"This one is twenty-one, brunette, and lives at 1619 Pine Street."

Mindy had been listening from the other room, and confronted the questioner. "Excuse me, but who are you and how do you know who I am?"

The customer was taken aback and tried to cover. "Oh, uh . . . the sign said McConnell's Music Store and . . . he said your name was Mindy."

"I did not," said Mork.

"Okay, I'll level with you. I'm from the *Boulder Evening Sun* – Clint Mullet, ace reporter."

"You don't act like a reporter," Mindy said suspiciously.

"Well," Clint said reluctantly, "I'm actually Clint Mullet, ace copyboy . . . but I'm just one scoop away from being a reporter! I'm working on a story so big that no other reporter would touch it. I'll come to the point, Miss McConnell: A few months ago, you were out on a date at Boulder Lake with one Bill Burns."

"That rat! We had a fight and he drove off stranding me." Mindy winked at Mork, remembering that this had been the night they had met.

"Did you see anything unusual that night?" Clint continued. "Like UFOs?"

Mindy shot a worried look at Mork, who laughed his Orkan laugh. *"Annhh! Annhh!* Do you believe in flying saucers?"

"Twelve people reported seeing glowing flying saucers that night," Clint went on. "How could you have missed it?"

"Uh, I'm afraid of the dark," Mindy offered. "I had my eyes closed. Now if you'll excuse me Mr. . . ."

"Mullet, Clint Mullet, the next Lou Grant. Good-bye." Clint left.

"Boy, that was a close call," said Mindy.

"I think he wants to be my friend," Mork answered.

"Well of *course* he does – it's you he's after!"

"Don't worry, Mindy. There's an old saying in hyperspace: Sometimes the best

place to hide from your enemy is right under his noses."

The next night, long after Mork was asleep, the window to Mindy's living room opened slowly. Clint Mullet climbed in, shining the light around the room to make sure it was empty. He then proceeded to search the room thoroughly, but managed to look right at Mork's space suit in the armoire without thinking anything amiss. Finally, he sat down on the couch, which let out a squeal. Terrified, Clint jumped up.

"Took you long enough to find me," said Mork warily. *Annhh! Annhh! Great game.*

Clint saw an opportunity to cover up what he had done. "Yes, that's it, Mork, I was playing a game with you. . . . No, wait, you're toying with me. You can see right through me, right?"

"No, you're opaque."

"Listen Mork, I'll level with you. I'm *sure* that Mindy knows something about that UFO sighting. Who knows — she may even have *met* one of those monsters. So I came here looking for clues."

"What sort of clues?"

"Well, it takes a trained eye to spot 'em. What's that, for instance?" Clint was pointing directly to Mork's space helmet. Then he lifted the helmet up, completely ignoring it, and took a folder from underneath it.

At that moment, Mindy and Fred, returning from a concert, walked in.

"Hi, Mindy," Mork chirped. "Clint and I were playing a new game."

"The only game I'm playing is 'catch the alien.' I have evidence right here that Mindy knows the leader of some planet called Ork."

Fred, Mindy and Mork looked at each other fearfully as Clint proudly held out the folder he had grabbed from under the helmet.

"See — right here, it says 'Orch leader.'"

Mindy laughed. "That's Dad's music."

"Look," said Fred. "It's O-R-C-H, that's an abbreviation for 'orchestra leader.' I'm leading the orchestra at the high school this weekend."

"That's the second game you've lost," Mork said. "You better start all over and come through the window again."

"You came in the window??!" Mindy was furious. "I've had enough of you. Get out of my house and never come back. Beat it!"

"Mindy," Clint began sheepishly, "I have an admission to make. You know the newspaper, *The American Inquirer?* Well, they're offering twenty-five thousand dollars for proof of an alien being living on earth. If you give me exclusive rights to the story, you can have the money — I'll settle for the fame. All you have to do is give me proof of an alien being."

The room fell silent. Fred and Mindy were looking to the ground, thinking hard. Mork looked worried. Could money be coming between Mork and Mindy?

A few minutes later, Mork had gone up to the attic to sleep while Fred and Mindy sat in the living room. "You know," began Fred, "I could sure use that twenty-five thousand dollar reward. . . ."

"Dad!"

"Oh, don't worry, I could never turn in Mork."

The attic stairs slowly and quietly swung down and Mork perched there, listening to their conversation.

"I have to admit, though," sighed Mindy. "It sure would be nice to have that kind of money. I could quit work and go to school full time."

"And I could pay the plumbing bills and get new furniture. . . ." said Fred.

"Well, it's pointless to think about it. We can't turn him in."

"You know something, though, Mindy—it's not just the money. We'd be famous. We know the first alien ever to land on Earth. But, you're right, we can't turn him in. Well, let's go home and see Cora."

As the two left the apartment, Mork had already decided what he was going to do. He waited five minutes, then followed them over to Cora's apartment.

"I've thought it over and I'm going to turn myself in."

Fred and Mindy were even more shocked by Mork's pronouncement than they were by his sudden arrival at Cora's.

Cora had gone into the shower a few minutes earlier.

"Mork, why would you do a crazy thing like that?" Fred asked.

"Mindy's my best friend and you're her father. I know you need the money."

"Mork, everybody needs money," Mindy pointed out.

"That's right," said Fred. "You don't have to do a thing like that. It's very generous of you, but it's not worth the price you'd have to pay."

"That's right," said Mindy. "You'd never have any privacy. They'll force you to become a celebrity. Everyone'll be saying "Na-No, Na-No.""

"And you don't know what the government will do," Fred added. "They may think you're a threat to our security and lock you up. They might . . . stick you in a bottle."

"Oh, no," moaned Mork. "My grandfather was a bottle. He died a broken man."

"There's a chance we may never see you again."

Mork was confused. "It looks like my future is no bed of raisins . . . but I want to help my friends. I'll have to think this under."

Cora walked in, disgustedly wringing out the bottom of her bathrobe, which was sopping wet. "The pipes are broken again, Freddie."

"That settles it," announced Mork. He picked up the phone and dialed a number. "Clint? Mork here. Listen, if you come to Mindy's apartment at noon tomorrow, I promise you'll see a real live alien being. "Bye."

Clint showed up five minutes early the next morning, brimming with excitement. "Where is he? Where's the alien being, Mork?"

Mork was up in the attic. "He's getting dressed, Clint. Here he comes now." Mork strode down the attic stairs in full Orkan regalia, red spacesuit and silver helmet.

"I am Mork from the planet Ork. My mission on Earth is to observe your primitive civilization and report back to my superiors."

Clint snickered. "Come on, Mork. Is this what you brought me over here for? Red pajamas and silver boots? You look like one of the O'Jays."

"But I'm an alien being."

"Look, Mork, I know you want the money—"

"No, I'll prove it. See that glass of water?" Mork stuck his finger in the glass and began to drink, Orkan-style.

Clint was stunned. "How did you—" He was interrupted as Mindy and Fred ran into the apartment. The two were dressed in ridiculous monster-from-outer-space-suits: Mindy's was that of a cat-creature while Fred had an astronaut's bubble-helmet.

"Greetings! I am Mindy, the catwoman from Mars! I was sent to observe this primitive planet."

"Now, wait a—" stammered Mork. "*I'm* the alien."

"I am Fredzo, from the planet Scherzo." He held out a deck of cards to Clint. "Go on, pick one, any card."

"Clint," Mork said angrily, "I don't know how to tell you this, but they're putting you on. I'm the only real alien in the room. Watch that pitcher!" Mork pointed his finger at a pitcher of water sitting on the wicker chest. He made a low noise and water began spurting from the pitcher. "How d'ya like *them iggles!*" he said cockily.

Mindy swaggered forward. "Big deal. Step aside. Watch the picture on the wall." She pointed at a watercolor and made a funny noise. The picture fell, to Mork's amazement.

Clint walked over to the picture. "Wait a second, there's a string!" He followed the string to its end — the left hand of Fredzo from Scherzo.

"Well, Mork," Mindy said, breezily, "he found us out. *Shazbot.*"

Clint stormed towards the door. "This is the most unconvincing group of 'aliens' I've ever seen. And Mork, you're the worst!" Clint slammed the door behind him.

"Now you'll never get the money for your store," Mork said sadly.

"We won't get it from finking on you," said Fred. "I know it must be hard for you, living so far away from home."

"I'm beginning to think I *am* home," Mork said quietly. "But I don't understand why you did this. You needed the money so badly."

"No, you don't understand," said Mindy, "Having you here is more important than any amount of money."

Mork fell to his knees and hugged their legs. As Mindy and Fred exchanged pained looks, Mork said, "Thank you, thank you, thank you, thank you, thank you. . . ."

MORK'S REPORT TO ORSON

Mork calling Orson. Come in, Orson.

I hear you, Mork. What are we going to talk about this week?

Well, Orson, my value on the Earth market is twenty-five thousand dollars.

How much is that in grebbles?

Zero point three.

I could get more for you on Neptune.

It's amazing what they'll pay for a snack.

Were the McConnells selling you? I thought they made their money by selling sounds.

The sound business has been very quiet. *Annhh! Annhh!*

Money seems to be important to Earth-lings.

I'll buy that. They bring it to a place called a 'bank.'

What happens at a bank?

You bring in your money, it meets other money, mates and makes more money. It's like a singles bar for cash.

Can anyone get it?

No, only rich people. Banks will give you money to buy a boat but not to buy food.

Why is that?

I think it's because food is harder to repossess. . . . Hey, Orson, don't take any wooden *grebbles.* This is Mork signing off from Boulder, Colorado. *Na-No, Na-No.*

Old Fears

It was on a gloriously sunny Sunday afternoon late in autumn that Mindy decided to teach Mork about a popular Earth ritual—the picnic. The two arrived at Fred and Cora's apartment at noon, seeing if those two wanted to join them.

"Hello, Mindy," said her father, ignoring Mork. "How are you, darling?"

"Fine," answered the Orkan.

"I wasn't talking to *you*. . . ."

"We're going to Boulder Lake, Daddy, I've got the sandwiches and hot chocolate."

"Yes, and I see Mork has the blanket and the"—Fred stared at a jar Mork was holding in his hands—"the pepper?"

"No, the ants," answered Mork.

"Mindy said no picnic was complete without them."

"Those ants are revolting," said Fred with distaste.

"No, they're not," Mork said brightly. "They're happy with their form of government. See? They're dancing."

"We came by," said Mindy, changing the subject, "to see if you and Grandma wanted to come along."

"I'd like to, honey, but your grandmother isn't feeling too well. You remember her friend, Barney? The one she plays gin rummy with? Well, he passed away Friday night. She's taking it pretty badly—especially since Barney was four years younger than she." Just then, Cora

"She just doesn't have many friends her own age. She's lonely," Fred replied.

Mork was surprised. "On my planet, the Elders have all the friends they want."

"It's a little different here," said Mindy. "Lots of people ignore their elders."

"But they're the ones with all the knowledge and experience," insisted Mork. "On Ork, the elders are always surrounded by young people. Oh well, if Mrs. Hudson's lonely, I want to help."

"That's sweet of you, Mork," said Mindy kindly. "But she needs someone her own age. I don't think you can help much."

Mork wasn't so sure.

Mork made a point of dropping by the music store the next day when he knew Eugene would be around. He found the little tyke emerging from his violin lesson, and they exchanged their private soul-handshake.

"Plasma! What it is!" Mork was one jive alien. "Eugene, let me ask you something."

"That's what I like about you," answered Eugene. "Everyone else is always telling me things. You're the only one who *asks* me stuff. What's happening?"

"Eugene, what do old people like to do?"

"Well, my mother's thirty-one. She likes to watch TV."

"No, I mean much older, like Mrs. Hudson."

"Oh . . . I don't think they have any fun . . . maybe it's a law. They hang out at museums and the park."

entered through the archway, still wearing her pajamas and bathrobe.

"Hi, Mrs. Hudson," Mork greeted her cheerfully. He held up an unstringed guitar Fred had been repairing. "Want to buy a guitar? No strings attached!" He waited for her usual warm response, but she answered listlessly with a faint smile.

"No, thank you, Mork. I was just looking for my glasses." Before anyone could tell her the glasses were perched on her head, Cora wandered out of the room.

"Poor Grandma," said Mindy, shaking her head. "I've never seen her so depressed."

"She's not herself at all," Fred agreed. "She hasn't even called me a wiener for three days."

"Why is Mrs. Hudson so sad?" Mork wondered.

"What's so special about those places?"

"They're free, Mork. They go to the park and feed the pigeons. Hey, I gotta split."

"Right on. Thanks for the info." Eugene left and did not hear Mork call after him, "Eugene! Who do they feed the pigeons to?"

Later that afternoon, Fred and Cora were closing up shop. As Fred put on his coat, Cora said, "You go ahead, I want to stay around here for a while." Fred nodded — he had been unsuccessfully trying to cheer up Cora all day — and left, passing an old man who walked into the store.

The old man looked around and said, "Hello, good looking." Without looking up from the counter, Cora replied, "I'm sorry, Mindy's not here."

"Who's Mindy? I'm talking to you, Brown Eyes."

For the first time, Cora realized she was being addressed. "Oh, can I help you?" She smiled for the first time all day.

"I'd like a harmonica," the old man said.

"In what key?"

"Uh, the key of J."

"They don't come in J. How about C?"

"How about dinner, Cutie?"

Cora feigned shock. "No, I . . . I couldn't."

"Well, guess I'll make like a banana and split."

"Where are you going?" she asked.
"The museum."

"You know," said Cora slyly, "I've never been to the museum."

"Well, c'mon then! Let's not keep the statues waiting. This time of year, fig leaves might be falling." Cora's face lit up and she grabbed her coat.

"Wait a second . . . I don't even know your name yet."

The old man looked down at his new harmonica. "Uh, Hohner . . . Bill Hohner. But my friends call me 'Marine Band.' Let's go!"

They did.

A few days later, Fred and Mindy watched Cora primping in a small mirror as she waited for Bill Hohner to pick her up. "Mindy," Fred teased, "our little girl is growing up."

"Oh, you two are impossible," kidded Cora, who was enjoying the attention.

"I think it's terrific, Grandma. You've been like a new woman these past few days."

"That's right, Cora. Mindy and I are dying to meet the man who's responsible for all of this." As if on cue, there was a knock at the door. Cora left the room to get her coat and Mindy opened the door to Bill Hohner.

"Hi, I'm Mindy, you must be Bill. This is my father—my grandmother's son-in-law—Frederick McConnell."

"Charmed," said Bill, who proceeded to kiss both Fred's and Mindy's hands.

"You know," said Fred, "you've made my mother-in-law very happy."

"Yeah," said Mindy, "she's like a kid again . . . and we really want to thank you for that, Bill."

"Well," the old man began cheerfully, "I'm glad I've made you so happy. And since you don't mind what's happening between Cora and me, I'll let you in on a little secret. . . ." Bill's eyes sparkled for a moment in a way that Mindy found vaguely familiar.

"Na-No, Na-No," said Bill Hohner—alias Mork.

That afternoon, Mindy was still fuming when Mork sheepishly returned from his lunch date with Cora. He was still wearing his old-man clothes but looked his proper age.

"Hold it right there, Casanova," she warned him.

"Who, me?"

"And don't try to get out of this by acting dumb."

"I'm not acting," Mork said defensively. "Mrs. Hudson and I had a lot of fun tonight. First we helped a boy scout cross the street. Then we played chicken with some kids on skateboards. We were real scamps."

"Mork, how could you *do* such a thing?"

"What, change my age? I used my Orkan age machine."

"I'm not talking about that. How could you do such a horrible thing to grandma?"

"Horrible?" Mork was confused. "Why is it horrible if it makes her so happy?"

"You're being unfair, Mork. She's a nice person, right?"

"Right."

"So she deserves another nice person to love her and make her happy. And what if she falls in love with you? You're not going to marry her, and that might break her heart. Mork, you could be doing more harm than good."

Mork cringed, realizing the mistake he had made. "I'm such a *nimnul! Engh-engh* to me! On my face!"

"Your intentions were good."

"We have a saying on my planet: the road to Earth is paved with good intentions."

"Well, you'll have to tell her you can't see her anymore."

"It's going to be hard," Mork said sadly. "I think she really likes that old man."

Mork arrived at Cora's for their date that night with grim resolve. After exchanging some pleasantries, they sat on the couch and he spoke solemnly.

"Cora, there's something I have to tell you."

"No, Bill, there's something I have to tell *you*."

"Well, pearls before swine. Go ahead."

"First of all, I want to thank you for helping me through a rough time."

Bill Hohner looked at his anklewatch. "Rough time? *Kayo*. It's about ten after eight."

Cora continued. "The other thing is that I want to say that I know who you are — Mork."

Mork was shocked. "How could you tell?"

"Oh, come on. The anklewatch. *Kayo*. And remember when we went to the museum and you admired that one piece?"

"Oh, yes, the lovely metallic sculpture."

"That was the air-conditioner."

"Boy, I'm a real *nimnul*. I guess you don't like me any more."

"Not like you? I like you more than ever before. You snapped me out of a blue funk, made me realize that I have a family that cares about me, a good job, and" — she looked into Mork's eyes — "friends of all ages. But there's one thing I don't understand: last night I kept tweaking your cheek to see if you were wearing make-up . . . but you weren't! There's no way on Earth you could have become an old man temporarily."

"You're beginning to get the idea. . . . Look, I'm going to tell you something, because I respect you and I think you're starting to catch on." He took a deep breath. "I'm a man from another planet."

"You want to hear something weird? I believe you. I suspected something like that when you carved our initials in that tree with your finger."

"I can drink with it too!"

"What a relief," said Cora. "Ever since you moved in with Mindy, I've been seeing things that made me think my mind was going. It's so simple . . . a man from outer space."

"You accept it so easily. Most people go crazy."

"Mork, I've been around a long time. I've seen the age of the automobile, the talking movies and a man on the moon. If we can go out there, there's no reason why you can't come here."

"Now we can go back to our right ages and be friends, right?"

"Absolutely. Let's shake."

After a pause, Cora asked Mork, seriously, "If you can make yourself older, can you make another person younger?"

"No," Mork said sadly.

Cora shook her head and began to laugh. "Shazbot!"

MORK'S REPORT TO ORSON

Mork calling Orson. Come in, Orson.
You sound tired, Mork.

I've been exercising. I aged myself and I'm still a little stiff.

You aged yourself? That's a cheap way to get respect.

It's not that way here, Orson. The young people get all the attention.

What do young people know? They don't have the experience. That doesn't make sense.

I don't understand it myself, Orson. Everything else on Earth gets more valuable as it gets older — wine, furniture, cheese, coins . . . everything but people.

The Earthlings ignore their ancient ones.

They don't do anything nice for them?

Oh, yes, they do one thing — they fix their incomes.

But why do they treat the Elders that way?

Well, I've heard that when people get older, they fall into a state of disrepair. Their hearing starts to fail.

Why is that, Mork?

Well, I have a theory. . . . I think it's because no one asks them anything. Such a waste. Well, this is Mork, signing off. *Na-No, Na-No.*

THE PROPER MANNER TO HANDSHAKE (NA-NO, NA NO) IN ONLY 6 STEPS.

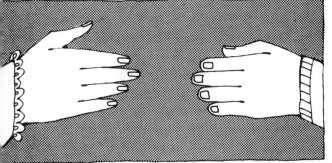

① Be sure each person has a hand to shake. (Preferably a hand should have five fingers.)

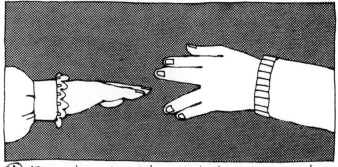

④ Female should rotate hand counter-clock-wise until palm is parallel to ground. With 2 females older one will rotate hand; with 2 males, the male with more chest hair will rotate.

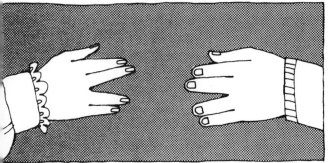

② Extend hand. Separate fingers so that index and middle fingers are together and ring and little finger are together.

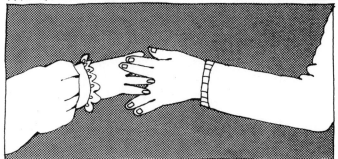

⑤ Interlock fingers in this position. Hold for at least 4 seconds and no more than 2 days.

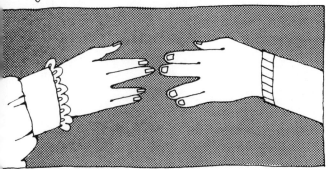

③ Reach hand out - (as if to touch) - stop when longest fingers are ⅛" apart. Flex hand muscles.

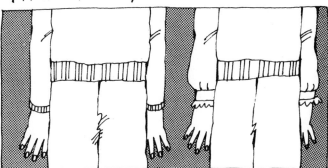

⑥ Relax hands. Lower arms to side. Feel free to move on and na-no, na-no to someone else.

INTERGALACTIC FLIGHT TICKET

form 8881200

ticket: XO52T   seat-22C (rotten view)

to: ork   from: earth

This ticket must be punched before boarding flight. This ticket is a one-way fare except for ex-nimnuls. When ticket is valid for return travel it must be presented to chief zeepslod by 9:24 P.M. Tickets held by right-handed persons not valid on peak hour flights. This ticket good on all flights except for Fridays falling on odd-numbered days.

THIS TICKET VOID IF NOT USED BEFORE 7·15·80
Departure gate: Q·O·Z·88

Fare: $2.46   meal: $39 extra

cut along the dotted line

118

The Great Mork & Mindy Trivia Test

The following trivia test is designed to test your knowledge of and allegiance to the historic tale of Mork and Mindy. All of the questions are of the multiple-choice variety. The idea is for you to choose the correct answer from the choices listed below each question.

The questions are divided into three categories of difficulty — basic, intermediate and advanced. Keep track of your answers, check them against the correct listings on page 124, and finally tally your score and rate yourself according to the chart on page 124.

SAMPLE

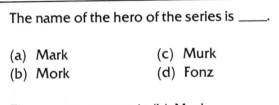

The name of the hero of the series is _____.

(a) Mark   (c) Murk
(b) Mork   (d) Fonz

The correct answer is (b) Mork.

SECTION ONE – BASIC   (20 POINTS)

Score one (1) point for each correct answer.

1. Mork arrives on Earth from the planet _____.
   (a) Keren
   (b) Neptune
   (c) Ork
   (d) Cootie

2. Mork's spaceship is shaped like a(n) _____.
   (a) barbell
   (b) thermos
   (c) egg
   (d) giraffe

3. Mork is sent to Earth as punishment because he _____.
   (a) didn't give his dog enough cheese
   (b) painted a mustache on the solar lander
   (c) knew too much
   (d) was too fat

4. The distance between Ork and Earth is _____.
   (a) 10 miles
   (b) 24 kilometers
   (c) 60 billion light years
   (d) more than you can shake a stick at

5. Mindy is _____ old.
   (a) 15 years
   (b) 21 years
   (c) much too
   (d) fifteen dog-years

6. Mindy works at McConnell's _____ Store.
   (a) General
   (b) Grocery
   (c) Liquor
   (d) Music

7. Cora is _____.
   (a) older than Fred but younger than Mindy
   (b) younger than Fred but older than Mork
   (c) younger than neither Fred nor Mindy
   (d) a spy for the CIA

8. *Mork and Mindy* takes place in _____.
   (a) Hendra, New Hampshire
   (b) Crist, Alabama
   (c) Boulder, Colorado
   (d) a shoe box

9. When Mindy first sees Mork, she thinks he is a(n) _____.
   (a) priest
   (b) boxcar tramp
   (c) idiot
   (d) rodent

10. The first time Mork is served coffee, he _____.
    (a) complains about its cost
    (b) sends it back to the kitchen
    (c) stares at it in terror
    (d) pours it on his cereal

11. Mork drinks orange juice with _____.
    (a) his finger
    (b) great style and dignity
    (c) a dash of ketchup
    (d) a side order of motor oil

12. Mork's mission on Earth is to _____.
    (a) destroy all life
    (b) observe our civilization
    (c) further the cause of the metric system
    (d) buy souvenirs and gaudy trinkets

13. Eugene is _____.
    (a) the capitol of Ork
    (b) a brand of deodorant
    (c) a black youngster studying the violin
    (d) Mork's pet *hibengie* on Ork

14. Cora calls Fred all of the following things except _____.
    (a) wiener
    (b) Fredzo
    (c) Joan of Arc
    (d) dumbo

15. Mork calls Orson all of the following things except _____.
    (a) Star Tush
    (b) Your Immenseness
    (c) Laser Breath
    (d) Grandma

16. The two most valuable commodities on Ork are _____.
    (a) death and taxes
    (b) fillies and mares
    (c) chocolate and vanilla
    (d) sand and dirt

17. Mork drives ____.
    (a) a 1955 Chevy
    (b) a *grembo pasati*
    (c) a Masarati
    (d) all of his friends to drink

18. Fred plays the ____.
    (a) ponies
    (b) field
    (c) trombone
    (d) fool

19. Mork communicates with Orson by ____.
    (a) telegraph
    (b) telepathy
    (c) telephone
    (d) Pony Express

20. Mindy wants a ____ degree.
    (a) journalism
    (b) third
    (c) Celsius
    (d) mail order

SECTION TWO – INTERMEDIATE (30 POINTS)

Score two points for each correct answer.

21. When Mork came to Earth on an earlier visit, he landed in _____ and met _____.
    (a) Yankee Stadium . . . Lou Gehrig and Bill Dickey.
    (b) Hollywood . . . Rin Tin Tin
    (c) a huff . . . with little acceptance
    (d) Milwaukee . . . Laverne DeFazio and Arthur Fonzarelli

22. Mork does an excellent imitation of ____.
    (a) Walter Winchell
    (b) Georgia O'Keefe
    (c) Seattle Slew
    (d) Ed McMahon

23. Exidor believes in ____.
    (a) high living, fast cars and cheap women
    (b) the transsubstantiation of the soul
    (c) intelligent life on Venus
    (d) the importance of maintaining diplomatic ties with China

24. Mork meets ____ and goes to work at ____.
    (a) a greyhound . . . the dog track
    (b) Hugh Hefner . . . building a bachelor pad
    (c) Rainbow Rappaport . . . The Vitamin Vendor
    (d) Abbott and Costello . . . a haunted house

25. When Mork becomes angry or frustrated, he says ____.
    (a) "Cerf's Up!"
    (b) *Shazbat!"*
    (c) "Aerosmith!"
    (d) *"Limakook!"*

26. Mork talks to all of the following except ____.
    (a) eggs
    (b) plants
    (c) plates
    (d) bankers

27. Mork's favorite TV show on Earth is ____.
    (a) *I Love Lucy*
    (b) *Petticoat Junction*
    (c) *Gilligan's Island*
    (d) *the test pattern*

28. *A splink* is a ____.
    (a) brand of *hibengie* food on Ork
    (b) stiff bandage used on broken fingers
    (c) a basin in the kitchen with hot and cold water
    (d) a practical joke

29. Exidor is the founder and President of ____.
    (a) General Motors
    (b) Tunisia
    (c) Friends of Venus
    (d) the world

30. Fred doesn't like being call Fredzo because ____.
    (a) it reminds him of his mother
    (b) It's such an unpleasant-sounding word
    (c) he feels he's not worthy of it
    (d) it sounds like the name of a detergent

31. Mork says the Venusians' only technological invention is ____.
    (a) the garbage can
    (b) the La-Z-Boy recliner
    (c) the frug
    (d) Szechuan food

32. Mork says all of the following cute things except ____.
    (a) "I'll stop bushing around the beat."
    (b) "I'll be up the Milky Way without a paddle."
    (c) "Is it soup yet?"
    (d) "I need time to think this under."

33. Mindy has dated all of the following men except ____.
    (a) Bill
    (b) Brad
    (c) Exidor
    (d) none of the above

34. The name Mork adopts as an old man is ____.
    (a) Maurice Chevalier
    (b) T. S. Crestvine
    (c) Bill Hohner
    (d) Orson Bean

35. Mork's gourmet dessert creation is ____.
    (a) A bologna sundae
    (b) a creme puff
    (c) *marrons eau de chien*
    (d) *shazbat*-flavored sherbet

PART THREE — ADVANCED   (50 POINTS)

Score five points for each correct answer.

36. Mindy's home address is ____.
    (a) 135 West 87th Street
    (b) 180 Riverside Drive
    (c) 1619 Pine Avenue
    (d) 44 Bow Street

37. Clint Mullet has been offered $25,000 to expose an alien by ____.
    (a) *The American Inquirer*
    (b) *The Harvard Lampoon*
    (c) *The Boulder Evening Sun*
    (d) *The Orkan Daily News*

38. Mork's father was ____.
    (a) Mr. Mork, Sr.
    (b) never ascertained by the authorities
    (c) an eyedropper
    (d) a sterile dish

39. Rainbow Rappaport will only drink ____.
    (a) soda
    (b) coffee
    (c) beer
    (d) water

40. Orkans usually stay *bezurb* for only ____.
    (a) thirty seconds
    (b) sixty seconds
    (c) five minutes
    (d) two *bleams*

41. A sign on Exidor's wall says, "On Mercury, call 955-3131, ask for ____.
    (a) Alice
    (b) Kerrie
    (c) Mary
    (d) Wanda

42. Mork's space suit is ____.
    (a) red, cotton and alive.
    (b) red, silver and furry.
    (c) blue, silver and alive
    (d) blue, red and furry.

43. An Orkan's two most erogenous zones are ____.
    (a) necks and earlobes
    (b) necks and wrists
    (c) earlobes and wrists
    (d) knees and wrists

44. Mork's favorite record to dance to is ____.
    (a) "Live at Leningrad Stadium"
    (b) "Mancini Goes Disco."
    (c) "Marcel Marceau's Greatest Hits"
    (d) "Howard, Phil and Kay's Greatest Hits"

45. The McConnells' landlords at the music store are ____.
    (a) Eddie and Adam Barbanel
    (b) Tom and Penny Daley
    (c) Arnold and Annie Wanker
    (d) Exceller and J. O. Tobin

Trivia Test Answers

1. c	16. d	31. a
2. c	17. b	32. c
3. b	18. c	33. c
4. c	19. b	34. c
5. b	20. a	35. a
6. d	21. d	36. c
7. c	22. a	37. a
8. c	23. c	38. c
9. a	24. c	39. c
10. d	25. b	40. b
11. a	26. d	41. c
12. b	27. a	42. a
13. c	28. d	43. c
14. c	29. c	44. c
15. d	30. d	45. c

Rate Yourself. Total up your points (1 for each correct answer, 1–20; 2 for each correct answer, 21–35; 5 for each correct answer, 36–45). A perfect score is 100.

0–20	*Hibengie*
20–40	*Nimnul*
41–60	Earthling
61–80	*Wurble*
81–100	Orkan
101 plus	Cheater

Glossary

A Basic Orkan Vocabulary

amrak: One of the noises an Orkan makes immediately after kissing an earthling.

aragato: Thank you.

brandel: An Orkan monetary unit; e.g., an in-stamatic glove costs as little as thirty *brandels.*

bleam: (Also spelled *bleem*). A measure of time on Ork, approximately equivalent to one Earth day.

beep-beep: Sound made by an Orkan after squeezing his nose, usually performed before going out to look for a job.

bez: The second number used in counting on Ork, presumably equal to the number "2" on Earth, but not necessarily so.

bezurb: A state of drunkenness or intoxication caused by drinking a carbonated beverage. See also *Ork-faced.*

cholly-cho-cho: Chin. Especially used in the idiom, "I wouldn't touch a *harf* on your *cholly-cho-cho.*"

coo-coo: Insane, deranged or crazy. Similar to English "cuckoo." See also *crathanza.*

crathanza: Deranged, insane or crazy. See also *coo-coo.*

Crilmuck: Jerk, nerd, *noid, spaz.* See also nimnul.

durkiss: A lively time, packed with all grab-bable gusto in sight.

Earthed up: To have done something wrong or to be *bezurb.* Derived from or similar to an equally obscene English idiom.

eenot: The third number used in counting on Ork, immediately following *bez* and preceding *gumbo.*

engh-engh: Woe, bad things or a curse, esp. as in the idiom, *"Engh-engh* to me! On my face!"

farging: A forbidden move practiced by un-scrupulous participants in a *holitacker.* The official rule is "No *farging* below the *smegas.*" See *holitacker.*

fif: An Orkan oil or lubricant, similar to *limakook* and *seve.*

flukie: Amusing puppet or doll used by an Orkan photographer, meant to induce proper eye focus and smiles in posing sub-jects. The idiomatic phrase is "Watch the *flukie!*"

frazh: A presumably large animal not ordinari-ly eaten; e.g., "I'm so hungry, I could eat a *frazh!*"

free: The sixth number used in counting on Ork, immediately following *gee* and preced-ing *infinity.*

frenkle: An Orkan life-form distinguished by an unusually long tail; e.g., "I'll be back in two shakes of a *frenkle's* tail!"

frez: The first number in counting on Ork, immediately preceding *bez.*

fribble: To scramble or confuse, esp. the brain; e.g., "My mind is really *fribbled.*"

gang neb: An Orkan sexual act, performed by a woman. The woman touches the man's wrist, occasioning him to say *"Zylabswitch, zeep, seep!"*

gazooba: A crawling, hairless form of Orkan animal life, considered more advanced than human beings.

gee: The fifth number used in counting on Ork, immediately following *gumbo* and preceding *free.*

gleek: An egg-shaked power-source or energizer. An Orkan must be recharged by his *gleek* every birthday, which falls only once every 2000 *zymes.*

glets: Orkan nonsense word.

grebbles: Orkan monetary units, each of which is equal to $83,333.33. In Earth money, $25,000 is equal to 0.3 *grebbles.*

grebengi: Nonsensical Orkan word.

gorgles: A state immediately before death on Ork. To "get the *gorgles*" means that one is about to die.

grembo pasati: A sporty Orkan roadster or automobile.

gumbo: The fourth number used in counting on Ork, immediately following *eenot* and preceding *gee.*

harf: A hair or other growth, sometimes found on the chin, and considered precious; e.g., "I wouldn't touch a *harf* on your *cholly-cho-cho.*"

hibengie: A common form of Orkan animal life which resembles a feather-duster.

holitacker: Mental competitions which take place instead of fistfights on Ork.

iggles: Used only in the cocky idiom, "How d'ya like *them iggles?*"

infinity: The seventh and final number used in counting on Ork, immediately following *free.*

kayo: Okay.

kerklenik: Word used to conclude business transactions, meaning "The deal is closed."

kraal: The sacrificial altar where the victims of *Volgar The Enforcer* are placed before the ritualistic tickling torture.

krell: Unit of time approximately equal to 7.3 years.

limakook: A lubricating oil indigenous to Ork, not unlike *fif* and *seve.*

loveling: Lover.

lurk: An Orkan measure of time, possibly equivalent to one Earth year.

Mork: A given name on the planet Ork, primarily used for males.

Na-No, Na-No: Na-No, Na-No.

nap, nap: A wrongdoing or forbidden act, similar to the English, "no-no."

nebits: An article of apparel which is removed as a gesture of respect; e.g., "I tip my *nebits* to you."

Necrotons: Enemies of the Orkans who were defeated by *Zippy the Bold* in a famous *holitacker* when *Zippy* yelled, "Hey! Your shoelaces are untied."

nelf: A species of Orkan vertebrate, distant relative of the *hibengie* and hairless *gazooba.*

new-new: A good event or sensation; e.g., "That's a spiffy *new-new!*"

nimmod: Loser, failure, reject, mutant. See also *crilmuck* and *nimnul.*

nimnul: Stupe, dummy,,idiot, wiener. See also *crilmuck* and *nimnod.*

noggachomps: Small animals which graze in Orkans' hair; the result is the equivalent of a haircut. Orkans often must set traps in their shorts to catch the persistent creatures.

onk: A face.

onk-onk: A squealing noise signifying pleasure or delight.

Ork: The planet Ork. *Frizbat* is the capital city, *gleeks* are the dominant form of transportation, and *holitackers* are used as a nonviolent form of settling arguments. Animal life includes the *hibengie, gazooba, frazh* and *noggachomps*.

Ork-faced: A state of drunkenness; e.g., "The minute those bubbles hit my bloodstream, I get *Ork-faced.*"

Orson: A man's given name on Ork.

pah-poo: Thank you. See also *aragato*.

ribbit: A handshake; i.e., a *ribbit* signifies *kerklenik*.

scrim: An imperative command meaning "leave the premises," similar to the English "scram!"

seve: An oily lubricant that shares common properties with *fif* and *limakook*.

shazbot: An exclamation of distaste or displeasure, named after what is often found under a *frenkle's* tail.

smegba: Area of the Orkan body below which no *farging* is allowed during a *holitacker*.

splinkling: Playing a practical joke on an Orkan or human.

swig: Lower Orkan life-form, distant cousin to the *nelf*.

syfnid: Hello.

Volgar: Volgar The Enforcer captures hapless Orkans, ties them to the sacrificial *kraal* and tickles them by candlelight. Before arriving, *Volgar* makes the noise of a harsh cuckoo clock.

wurble: A swell fellow, a great guy, a real prince, the *hibengie's* meow.

zabah: An exclamation of surprise.

zabodi: Orkan word, part of speech unknown, meaning obscure.

zazbak: See *zabodi*.

zazbat: Not playing with a full deck. See also *coo-coo* and *crathanza*.

zerks: Units used in measuring distance, similar to the English "foot."

zibby-dibby-do-wap-wee: Orkan expression of contentment or pleasure.

Zippy the Bold: The greatest Orkan warrior, conqueror of the Necrotons in the great *holitacker*.

ziz-bah: Noise made by an Orkan while exercising; i.e., while doing pull-downs.

zymes: A unit of time on Ork. An Orkan celebrates his birthday every 2000 *zymes*, and must recharge from his *gleek* or he will get the *gorgles*.